MACRAMÉ
WEAVING
AND
TAPESTRY

MACRAMÉ WEAVING AND TAPESTRY

Art in Fiber

Spencer Dépas

MACMILLAN PUBLISHING CO., INC.

NEW YORK

COLLIER MACMILLAN PUBLISHERS

LONDON

Macmillan Publishing Co., Inc.
866 Third Avenue, New York, N.Y. 10022
Collier-Macmillan Canada Ltd., Toronto, Ontario

Library of Congress Catalog Card Number: 72-80912

First Printing

Printed in the United States of America

To Rosalind and Sophie—
my wife and daughter

Contents

Color Illustrations

Plates may be found between pages 48 and 49.

Preface

This is a practical book. I have tried to combine the methods and techniques that have worked well in my classes and the ideas I have developed working independently as an artist in the textile area. It is my hope that this book will be a useful tool to help the reader easily and quickly develop his own sense of texture, line, and space as they relate to fibers, fabrics, and textiles.

The *Macramé* section assumes no prior knowledge of knotting. It begins with the basic knots. Macramé appears deceptively easy, but it can be quite complex and difficult to perfect. The difference between activity and art is the difference between knotting and macramé. I have tried to start at the beginning of macramé as an art form and stress the combination of knots in an ever-widening and more diverse context. Of course, this philosophy is my own—that of a macramé artist who has developed the use of large pieces of macramé as a definition of area.

The *Weaving* section assumes some basic knowledge of weaving. However, I have reviewed some of the techniques of dressing and warping the loom. If the reader is unfamiliar with weaving, perhaps it would be best for him to use one of the many excellent weaving texts that are available: *New Key to Weaving*, by Mary Black, and *Byways in Handweaving*, by Mary Atwater. Both are published by The Macmillan Company and are standard references used by many weavers.

Chapter 8 deals with the combination of the two textile forms: macramé and weaving. The two are often used together as they complement each other. When appropriately displayed, the special beauty of one form is accented by that of the other.

The *Tapestry and Double Weave* section develops a number of tapestry techniques and also explores leno weaving. Chapter 10 discusses the many possibilities of using double weave in wall hangings. One new technique is the use of double weave to make a tapestry which is described in the same chapter.

A feature unique to this book is the description of how to make the large macramé wall hangings for which I am well known. Up to the present, my technique has been a closely guarded secret.

My hope in writing *Macramé, Weaving, and Tapestry* is to present textiles as a workable, attractive medium for artists. This is part of my own approach, and I hope that it will become part of the techniques of my readers and students. In this approach is the fun of creation, the joy of seeing an idea become something of beauty, and a new way of seeing line, color, and space. I hope that working with macramé, weaving, and tapestry will make life and living more satisfying to my readers.

Acknowledgments

I would like to thank my students and friends: Phyllis Goldrick, Elaine Eckman, Karen Eckman, and Elliot Kriss, who contributed photographs; Yvonne Forbach, Hannele Heikkinen, Sandra Yvonne Baker, and Luckner Lazard, my countryman and a fine artist who contributed the line drawings; Arlene Kukafka and Lili Blumenau, a friend and great craftsman who is an outstanding weaver and tapestry artist. Their help and the contribution of their work, photographs, drawings, and modeling of macramé pieces are very much appreciated.

My appreciation also to Mary Autry, Elizabeth Ball, Hilda Breed, Peter Collingwood, Myriam Gilby, Joyce Griffiths, Maria and A. J. Halder, Mike Halsey, Robin Hardiman, David Holbourne, Theo Moorman, Sax Shaw, Lore Youngmark, and the many others who allowed me to use pictures of their work. Some of these craftsmen are English and some are Australian. It was most gratifying to have such international collaboration.

And my special thanks to my wife, Rosalind, who typed, edited, and helped to organize my material. Without Rosalind's help, this book would not have been possible.

Mon art . . .

Aujourd'hui je ne voudrais pas en parler, je serais trop long, tout en risquant de ne satisfaire à la fois tout un chacun.

D'aucun disent que je suis un peintre surréaliste—abstrait. D'autres affirment que je fais du cubisme—Suis-je Sculpteur, Peintre, Tisseur, Macramiste . . . comme l'on voudra.

Pour ma part je dirais que je suis (l'Artiste tout court) je transforme les couleurs, les mouvements, et impose une retraite à un passé audacieux, aux formes et couleurs d'autrefois.

> Peignez si vous pouvez
> Critiquez si vous voulez
> Chaque chose à son genre
> Chaque personne à sa façon

et Gide confie: « Tout ce que tu gardes en toi de connaissances distinctes restera distinct de toi jusqu'à la consommation des siècles . . . Pourquoi y attaches-tu tant de prix. »

SPENCER DÉPAS

My Art . . .

I won't speak of it today; I would go on at length, at the risk of satisfying no one.

Some say I am a surrealist-abstractionist. Others say I am a cubist. What does it matter. I am a sculptor, painter, weaver, macramist—as you wish.

For my part, I would simply say that I am an artist. I transform color and movement, retreating from a formidable past tradition while espousing its forms and colors.

> Paint if you can
> Criticize if you will
> Each item to its own kind
> Each person to his own methods

As Gide remarked, "All the special knowledge that you have will remain unique to you until the end of time . . . Why then render it so much value."

SPENCER DÉPAS

PART ONE

Macramé

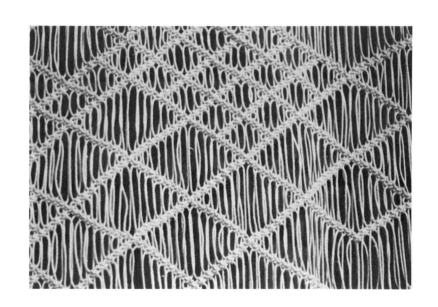

1

GETTING STARTED

Introduction:
A New Use of Texture,
Line, and Space

ACRAMÉ, the art of knotting, has been rediscovered as a challenge to hobbyists, artists, and craftsmen of today. During the past few years, thousands of people—young people, doctors, businessmen, housewives, and many others—have tried this ancient and timeless craft.

In America, macramé is often known as Square Knotting. This is a sailor's term. Until recently, it was usually sailors who practiced this craft. Macramé probably originated in the Near East many hundreds, if not thousands, of years ago. It was known in India and the Orient and may have been brought to the Western Hemisphere by the sailors of Columbus. *The Random House Dictionary* defines macramé as "knotted cotton trimming usually in a geometric pattern." The dictionary also tells us that the French word *macramé* is derived from the Turkish *makrama* meaning a face towel. This derivation indicates that macramé was originally a kind of edging, rather like the fringing often seen on today's towels. However, macramé is far more than just a trimming, even though it can be a superb edging for handwoven articles.

3

FIG. 1. *Inside my studio. A large macramé wall hanging is in back of the warping frame.*

In Central America and the West Indies, macramé is much used for making belts, handbags, and other small decorative objects. As a child in Haiti, I was taught how to make macramé belts at school. Not only can small articles such as belts be made of macramé, it can also be used as a technique for producing magnificent wall hangings—hangings where the division of line and space involves the use of macramé as an art form. Once the basic knots have been mastered, even the beginner can make large or small pieces that express his creative ability and aesthetic judgments.

In our small modern homes and functional apartments, space is at a premium. Because of this, macramé wall hangings and room dividers have become increasingly popular. These textile forms are ideal for an economical, decorative, and flexible use of area and color. Macramé, as a craft technique, can provide the individuality and expression of uniqueness that is so important in our mass-production oriented, technological society.

There are other ways of discovering new textural and visual avenues. These are discussed in the chapters on tapestry and other types of weaving. Perhaps the most exciting possibilities are in the combining of weaving with macramé. There is great scope here for the craftsman.

The sections on weaving assume an elementary knowledge on the part of the reader. This book does not teach warping, chaining, preparing the filling, making drafts, frame loom or

4

four-harness loom weaving. However, full instructions for tapestry weaving and leno are given.

The novice and advanced weaver are encouraged to explore new techniques, and to combine a variety of methods and materials. The advanced weaver will also find much to stimulate him, for as he acquires a knowledge of macramé, he will discover the great wealth of possibilities that exist for combining crafts to create new visual vistas and satisfactions.

Equipment and Materials

twine or cord—(use about 3 yards for practice)

wood—one piece, about 2 or 3 inches wide, ¾-inch thick, and about 20 inches long.

C-clamps (two)—a C-clamp is shaped like the letter "C." Pressure is obtained by means of a thumb screw, and the open section of the clamp is enlarged or diminished by use of the screw. Numbers 5, 6, and 9 are the most convenient sizes. C-clamps can be bought in hardware stores, and very often, they can be found in a five-and-ten-cent store.

finishing nails (one box of one-inch nails)—these nails are often called brads. They are long slender wire nails with very small heads.

hammer—either a metalworking or woodworking hammer will do. In fact, any instrument for driving the finishing nails into the wood is fine.

scissors—ordinary paper shears or all-purpose household scissors are excellent.

table—the table should be very sturdy. A card table will not work. A strong kitchen table is best.

You need very little preparation to make your first knot. Take the piece of wood and, using the clamps so that the thumb screws are pointing down to the floor, clamp the wood flat against the surface of the table. The wood is used only to protect the surface of the table, and the clamps are used only to secure the wood. If you have an old wooden table, or an old windowsill that you don't mind damaging, it can be used instead of the table, wood, and clamps.

Using the hammer and a few of the finishing nails, hammer a row of nails into the piece of wood, spacing the nails about three inches apart. The row of nails should be in the middle of the piece of wood, and each nail should stick up about three quarters of an inch.

FIG. 2. *The basic equipment for macramé: a piece of wood; two C-clamps; scissors; a hammer; pliers for pulling small-headed nails; and a box of finishing nails. Almost any kind of twine can be used for macramé.*

FIG. 3. *Some of the most popular twines used for macramé:*
a. Fisherman's Twine No. 15
b. Fisherman's Twine No. 18
c. Fisherman's Twine No. 30
d. Fisherman's Twine No. 35
e. Venetian Blind Cord
f. Laundry Line Cord
g. Sisal, medium
h. Sisal, heavy
These twines are all available at most five-and-ten-cent stores. Hardware shops also carry interesting cord and twine.

Now to start working with the cord: I suggest fisherman's twine as the best to use for macramé. My favorite sizes are Numbers 16, 20, and 30 (fig. 1). You can also use silk, rayon, or sisal cord, or any other twine or cord that is easily available. Beginners often find that it is best to use a medium cord (No. 30) until they master the knot.

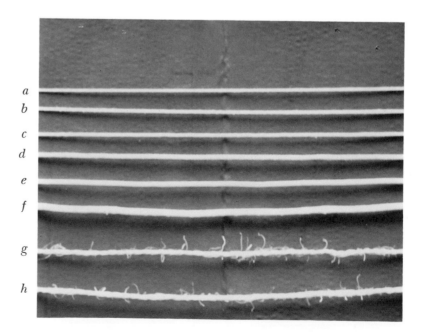

2

TYING THE
BASIC KNOT

THE best way to begin macramé is to start by making a cord of Square Knots. Such a cord is called a sennit—an old nautical term meaning a braided or knotted cord (fig. 4). You'll need string or twine, scissors, wood, nails, clamps, and a hammer.

Cut two long pieces of twine. Each piece should measure about 6 yards (18 feet) long. The best twine to start with is Number 20 or 30, or if you prefer, Number 18 fisherman's twine.

Double each string so that it forms a loop at one end, and then tie the loop with a knot (fig. 5). Nail both doubled strings

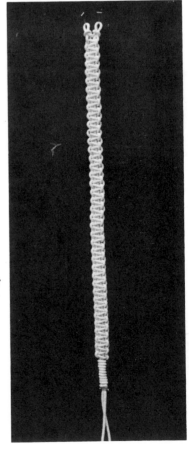

Fig. 4. *A sennit, or knotted cord, made of the basic Square Knot.*

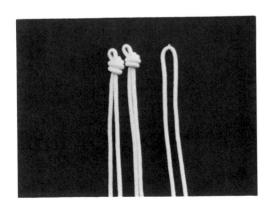
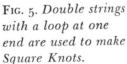

Fig. 5. *Double strings with a loop at one end are used to make Square Knots.*

to the wood; use a one-inch finishing nail at the end of the loop so that the doubled strings are next to each other and there are four ends of string. Be sure to hammer the nail securely into the wood so that the strings will hold, even if there is some tugging and pressure as you tie the knots.

WAIST STRING

Tie a piece of string around your waist with a bowknot— the same kind of knot that you use to tie your shoelace (figs. 6 and 7). Slide the bow to the back so that it will not get in your way, and you will have a smooth belt of string around your waist in front.

Now select the two middle strings from the four ends (fig. 8) and tie these two middle strings to your waist string (figs. 8, 9, and 10). While you are making the knot, your body must keep the tension on the middle strings just as if your hand were holding the two strings (fig. 8).

After tying the two center strings to your waist string, move back in your chair slightly to make the strings attached to your waist straight and taut. Try to control their tension by pulling yourself forward or backward to get just the correct amount of slack or pressure.

FIG. 6. *Left, A waist string makes knotting a lot easier.*

FIG. 7. *Right, The waist string tied with a bow.*

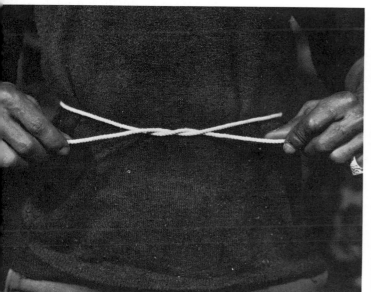
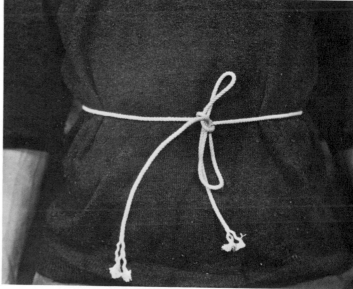

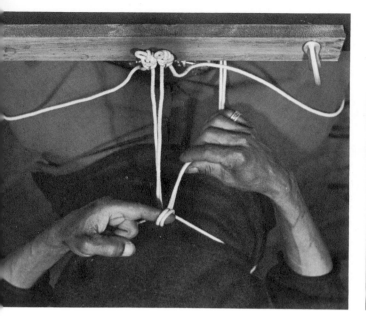
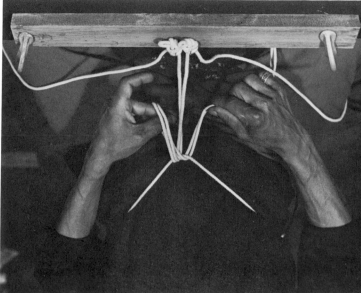
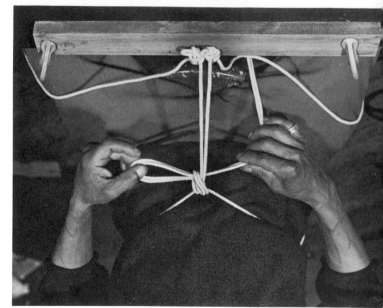

FIG. 8. *The double strings have been nailed to the board. The two middle strings are to be attached to the waist string.*

FIG. 9. *The two middle strings must be securely attached but easily undone. Loop them over the waist string.*

FIG. 10. *Starting to make a Square Knot.*

TYING THE FIRST KNOT

Take your right-hand string (the fourth string from the left —see fig. 11) and make a loop with the first two fingers of your left hand. Place the loop on top of the two middle strings— the strings that are tied to your waist string (fig. 11) while still holding the loop ends with the index finger and thumb of the right hand. At the same time, the index finger and thumb of the left hand should be inside the loop (fig. 12).

9

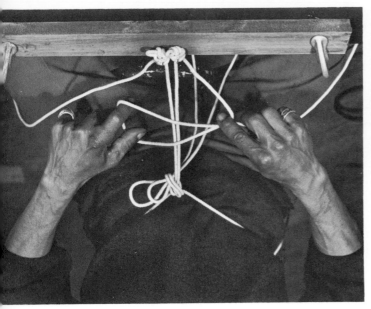

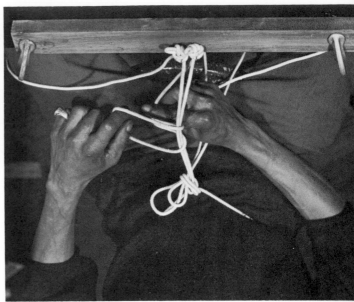

FIG. 11. *Left, Holding the loop in the first two fingers of your left hand.*

FIG. 12. *Right, Bend the loop downward with the left hand and catch the string, now held by your right hand, with the thumb and index finger of your left hand.*

FIG. 13. *Left, A double loop within a loop.*

FIG. 14. *Right, Pull the left-hand string through the double loop.*

Bend both hands slightly downward, but keep them above the two middle strings so that the two fingers which are in the loop can take the strings from the loop underneath the two middle strings (fig. 13). Pull a little so that the knot forms two loops (fig. 14). Put the left thumb inside the two loops to hold them until you pass the first string on your left-hand side (figs. 14 and 15) through the two loops (fig. 16). After pulling the first string through, you will notice a kind of arch underneath (fig. 17). Hold the arch with your left hand, and the fourth string with the right hand (fig. 17), and pull slightly, as shown in figure 18.

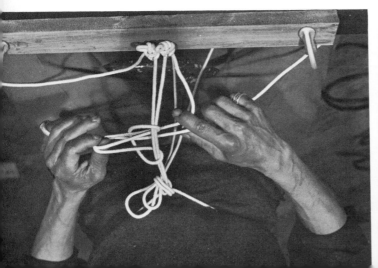

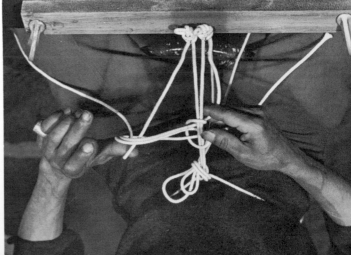

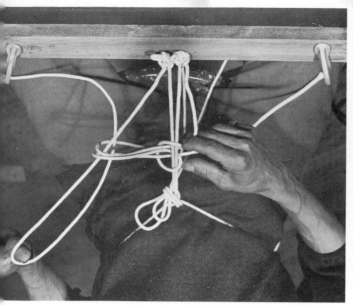

FIG. 15. *The left-hand string going through.*

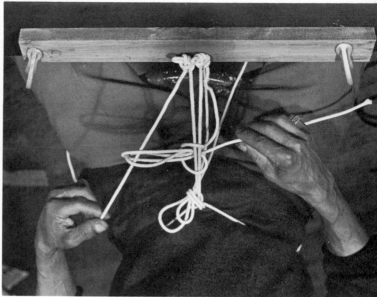

FIG. 16. *The left-hand string all the way through.*

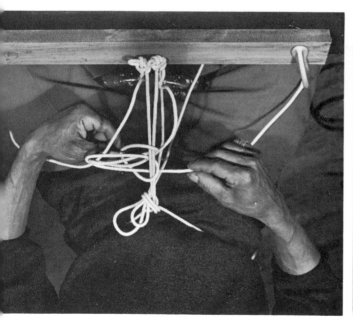

FIG. 17. *Adjusting the underloop.*

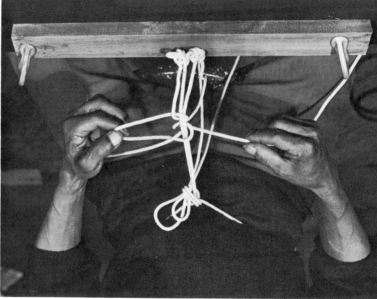

FIG. 18. *Two knots are starting to appear.*

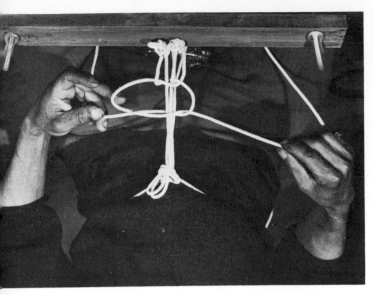

FIG. 19. *The two knots.* FIG. 20. *Tie one knot at a time.*

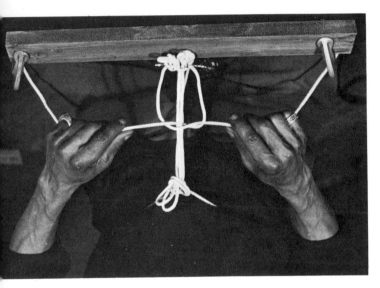
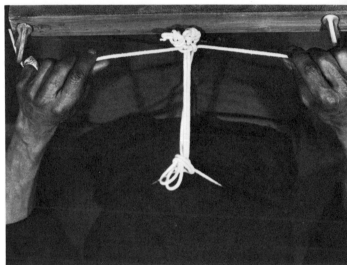

FIG. 21. *Tying the second knot near the first.* FIG. 22. *A finished Square Knot.*

As you are pulling the fourth string and the arch, move both hands backward and forward. When you do this, you will notice that two knots are formed (fig. 19) which should then be tied tight, one at a time (see figures 22 through 24). Figure 22 shows your first Square Knot and figure 23 illustrates the Square Knot in line drawings. Continue by repeating the Square Knots until your string is almost used up (figs. 24 and 25).

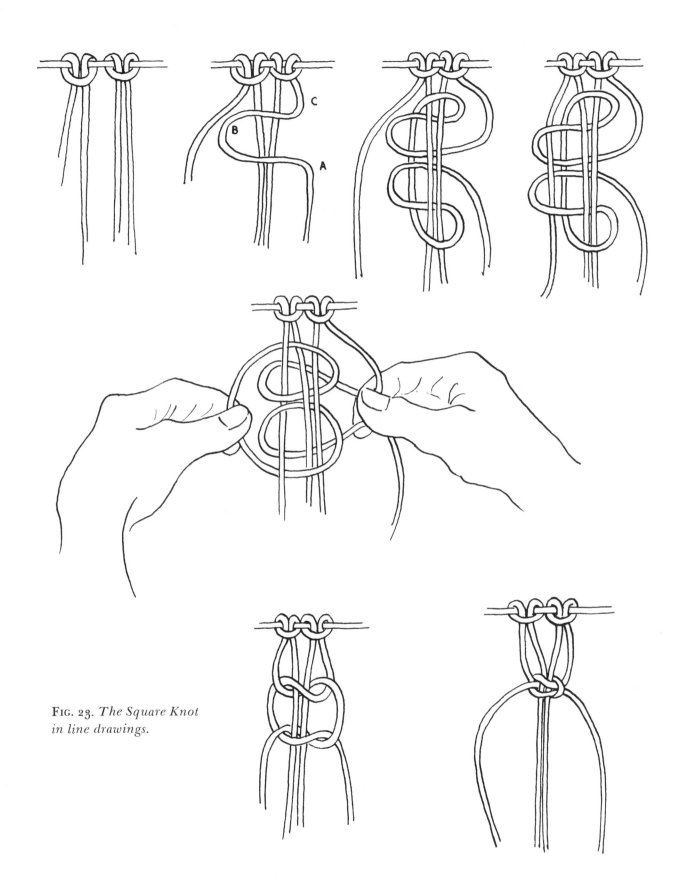

FIG. 23. *The Square Knot in line drawings.*

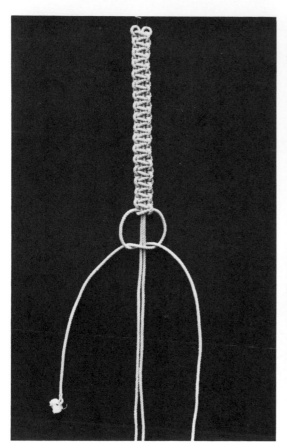

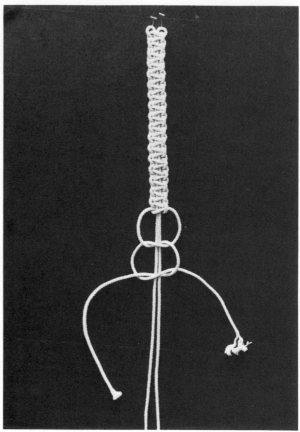

FIG. 24. *A sennit of Square Knots.*

FIG. 25. *Almost ready to finish the Square Knot sennit.*

FINISHING

To finish your first project, you can leave the ends loose, or you can select either the first or fourth string—either one of the outside strings—and twist it around the other three strings, binding them tightly together until you reach the end of the sennit. You can sew the end with a needle or glue it with cement glue. Epoxy glue will hold the twine, and it is almost invisible when it is dry. An example of this type of finish is shown in figure 4.

Another way to finish the sennit is to leave two or three strings and bind the others. If you choose to have only two, cut the third string short and cover the remaining two with the binding string as you twist it around the first string.

After you have practiced the single Square Knot and you feel confident when you make that knot, you are about ready to make the belt shown in figure 26.

For this project you will need much more cord or twine than you used for the first sennit. You will need 8 double strings —8 double strings means 16 ends, and each of those ends should be from 3 to 3½ times the length of the finished belt, varying according to your design.

MEASURING TWINE

Let's begin by planning a belt that will use 16 ends, each of which should be about three times the length of the finished belt. For example, if your belt is going to be 28 inches long (remember to allow for a closure and some overlap) you will need 28 times 3 for each end, or 84 inches for each of the string ends. There will be 8 strings that are doubled to make the 16 ends, so the total length of string you need is 1,344 inches:

> 8 strings doubled (8 × 2) = 16 ends
> each string end = 84 inches
> 16 (the number of ends) × 84 = 1,344 inches

1,344 inches equals 112 feet, or about 40 yards. Macramé does take a great deal of string!

Let's measure again; this time for another belt. Pretend you want to make a belt 26 inches long, and again use 16 ends (8 doubled strings). Here is how you could calculate the amount of string you would need:

> Each end must be 3 times 26 inches.
>   3 × 26 = 78 inches
> You will need eight doubled strings.
>   8 inches × 78 inches = 1,152 inches
> To make a belt of 16 ends that will be 26 inches long, you
>   will need 1,152 inches of twine.

Measuring the long lengths of cord or twine can be tricky. To measure the cord more easily, you can use your two clamps, or two long nails, or pegs, or the backs of chairs. Fix your

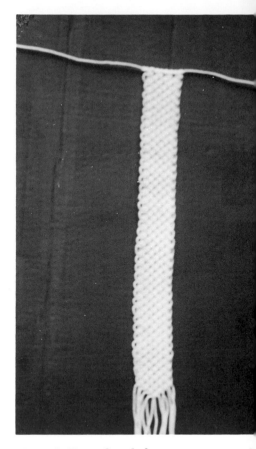

FIG. 26. *Your first belt, knotted, pointed, and ready to finish.*

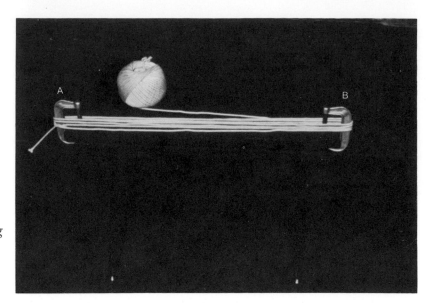

FIG. 27. *Table set up with clamps used for measuring string.*

clamp or nails to one end (A) of a long table, windowsill, or any other suitable piece of wood, as shown in figure 27. Measure your cord or twine for one string end. If you were making the 26-inch belt, the string would measure 78 inches (remember to double, because each of the 16 ends comes from 8 strings doubled) times 2, or 156 inches.

Start by attaching the string to A and then reel the twine out, measuring 78 inches, to B. Go around B, and reel the twine back to A, making a double strand. Now you have two of the 16 ends. Continue going from A to B and back to A, reeling out the twine as you go. Do this seven more times, for a total of eight cords around the posts or clamps. Be sure to end at A, the point where you started, so that all the string will be doubled. For this project you need 8 double strings. Cut the ends at A so that they come loose, but leave the ends uncut at B. You will now have 8 double pieces of string of the correct length, with a loop at the middle of each piece of string, making 16 ends.

Now take another piece of string approximately 10 inches long (A–B in fig. 28). Take each double piece of string, one at a time, and lay the loop over the short piece of string A–B (step 1, fig. 28). Bend the loop down backward behind the short string (step 2) and then draw the two long loose ends through the loop. The loop will be in front as in step 3, figure 28. Then pull the string tight (step 4, fig. 28).

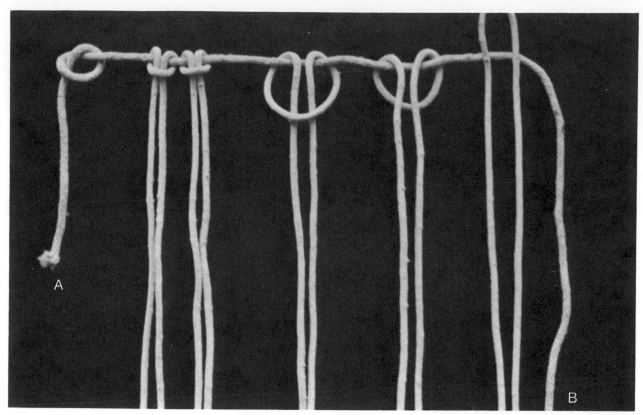

FIG. 28. *Loops attached to a short piece of string (A–B).*

KNOTTING THE BELT

Now to make your first belt. Don't forget that you need 4 strings for each Square Knot, so you are going to use 8 double strings, just as in figure 29. Eight double strings will give you 16 ends.

You are going to make the Square Knots as you did for your first project (p. 7). Select the first four ends of string, starting from the left, and start working toward the right—the same direction that you read. Take the two middle strings, 2 and 3, and attach them to your waist string or waist hook. (A waist hook is a small wood and metal hook or metal hook that attaches to the waist string or belt. The waist hook holds the middle strings as you work, just as they would be held if you had knotted them over the waist string. You can buy waist hooks at some macramé supply stores. I don't bother to use them, but many people find them convenient.)

Make the first knot as you did before, as shown in figures 14 through 25. After you have finished the first Square Knot, detach the two middle strings (2 and 3) from your waist and then take the next four strings, from left to right (numbers

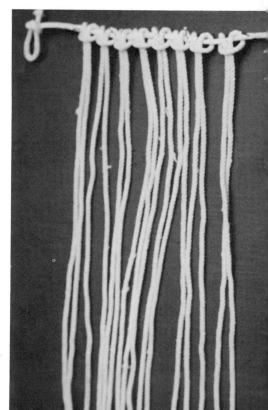

FIG. 29. *Eight double strings knotted over a shorter string to make 16 ends.*

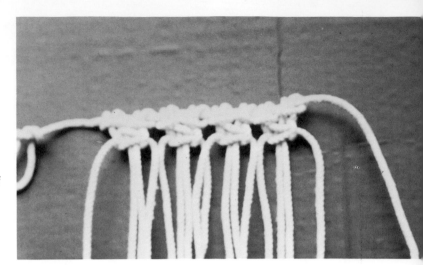

FIG. 30. *The first row of Square Knots.*

5, 6, 7, and 8) and make the knot just as you did the first one. After that knot is complete, release the two middle strings (6 and 7) from your waist, and continue to make the third knot, using strings 9, 10, 11, and 12; then the fourth knot with strings 13, 14, 15, and 16 (fig. 30).

THE SECOND ROW

You now have four Square Knots next to each other. You must attach or put them together to form a unit. To do this, push the first knot toward the second knot. Then select strings 3, 4, 5, and 6 (counting from left to right) to make the first knot on the second row. Use strings 4 and 5 for the two middle strings to attach to your waist and use 3 and 6 to tie the Square Knot. When you've completed the first knot of the second row, release yourself from the first knot to make the second knot of the second row. Select strings 7, 8, 9, 10 and attach numbers 8 and 9 to your waist. Make the second knot and release yourself again. To make the third knot, use strings 11, 12, 13, and 14. After you have made this knot, your second row is finished. Notice that there are four Square Knots on the first row, but only three on the second row. (See figure 31.)

The third row is made exactly like the first row. For the first knot, you use strings 1, 2, 3, and 4, for the second knot, strings 5, 6, 7, and 8, for the third knot, strings 9, 10, 11, and 12, and for the fourth knot, strings 13, 14, 15, and 16 (see figure 32).

Keep working in this way until your belt is as long as you want it to be. Make sure that you tie your knots straight, especially at the sides, so that each row is even, and your work does not go crooked. One way of getting even knots is to always sit

18

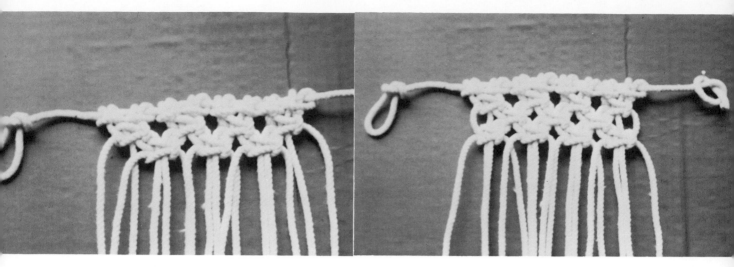

FIG. 31. *The second row of Square Knots.*   FIG. 32. *The third row of Square Knots.*

directly in front of the knot you are tying. If you are directly
opposite the knot you tie, it will come out much more evenly.

FINISHING

Before you finish your belt, it should be shaped to a point
at the end. After it is shaped to a point, the knots must be
secured in such a way that they do not unravel. The shaping
and finishing gives the belt an attractive professional look. Let
us proceed step-by-step to learn this technique, so that you will
be able to finish any belt that you make. Do you remember that
when you started the belt you had four knots on the first row?
(See p. 18.) In the second row there were only three knots. In
other words, you dropped two strings on each side of the second
row so that the knots would hold together. If you want a pointed
end to your belt, you must continue to drop the string ends
on each side.

After you have done a second row of three knots, proceed
to row three, but instead of making four knots as you did in
row one, or three knots as in row two, make only two knots.
The first knot on row three should be made with strings 5, 6,
7, and 8. The second knot on row three should be make with
strings 9, 10, 11, and 12. After this, you are ready to make the
knot on row four, which has only one knot. To bring your belt
to a point, take strings 7, 8, 9, and 10 and attach strings 8 and 9
to your waist string. Make a Square Knot as usual. You will

then have a nice pointed shape to the end of your belt (fig. 33). You will also have a fringe of strings around the pointed shape.

Study the work that you have done so far, and you will notice that on each row of Square Knots you have dropped two strings on each side of your belt to make the pointed shape. To secure the end so that it does not unravel, you must proceed in the following way.

THE DOUBLE HALF HITCH

The principle of the Double Half Hitch is that you bring the two outside strings of the belt to the center by making a series of Double Half Hitches on each side. Start on the right side (fig. 35). Take the last string, number 16, with your left hand. Then take string 15 and hold it with the index finger of your left hand on the left of string 16. Pass string 15 underneath string 16, then over it and down through the loop formed between strings 15 and 16 and pull the loop tight. (See figures 35, 36, and 37.)

Repeat the same procedure once more with the same strings (15 and 16) because you need two Double Half Hitches (fig. 39). After you have finished this, leave string 15 hanging down and keep string 16 in your left hand. Take string 14 in your right hand, bring it underneath string 16, then over it, then inside the loop between strings 14 and 16, as before, and tie the knot tight. Next, repeat the Double Half Hitch, using the same strings as before (strings 14 and 16). Repeat the same two Double Half Hitches with each string until you reach string number 9, which is the middle of your belt.

At this point, you stop and start again from the left side

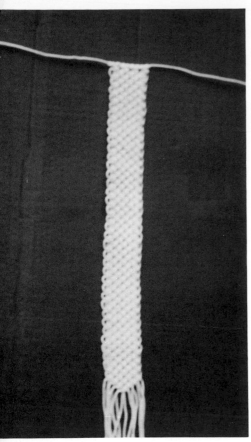

FIG. 33. *A belt finished with a pointed end. Double Half Hitch knots were used to prevent unraveling.*

FIG. 34. *Work from the right to the middle when you start a Double Half Hitch.*

20

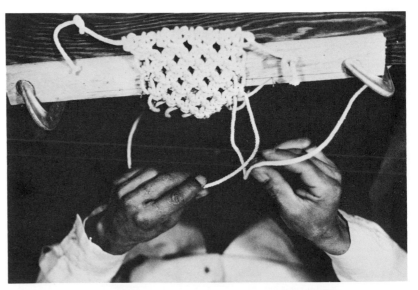

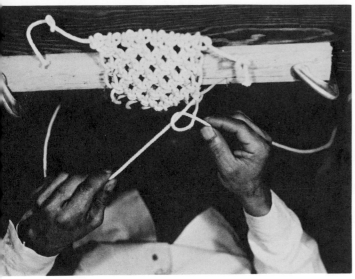

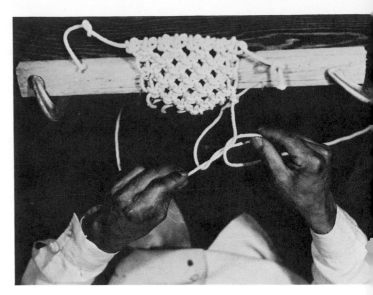

FIG. 35 FIG. 36

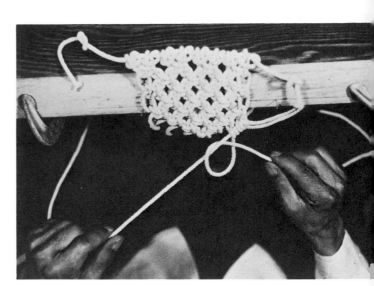

FIG. 37 FIG. 38

(fig. 39). This time use string 1 and continue in such a way that eventually string 1 will meet with string 16 at the center of the belt. You must proceed as you did for the right side of the belt, but instead of holding string 1 with your left hand, you must hold it with your right hand. You take the number 2 string, hold it with the index finger of the right hand, on the right side of string 1. You then pass string 2 underneath string

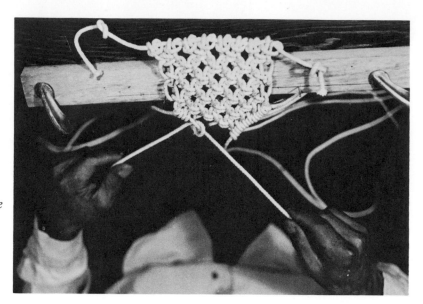

FIG. 39. *Starting from the left side and working toward the middle.*

1, over it, down through the loop between strings 1 and 2, and pull it tight. Make another Double Half Hitch in the same way with the same strings. Next, take string number 3, and while still holding string 1 as you did before, pass string 3 underneath string 1, over it, and down inside the loop between strings 3 and 1. Continue making knots in this way until string 1 meets string 16 at the center. Your last Double Half Hitch should be made with strings 1 and 16 as they meet (fig. 40). Tie strings 1 and 16 again so that they do not unravel. You can now leave the ends loose or cut them short, and they will not unravel.

Study each row of knots again. All the knots should be parallel to each other. Also, when you tie a knot, it should always be tied in the same way and with the same tension that you tied the preceding one. In this way, the first knot will be at the same level as the second, third, fourth, and so on.

FIG. 40. *Meeting at the middle with a knot that will secure the finished belt.*

22

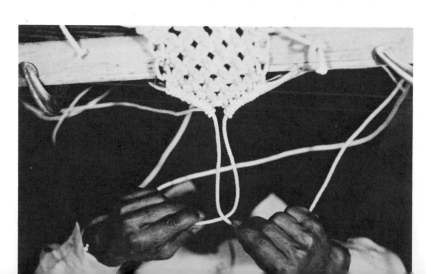

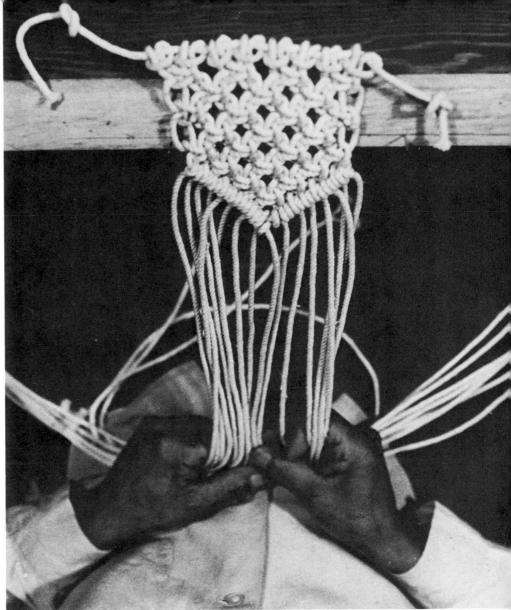

When knots are tied properly in a single knot project, such as the belt that has been described, you can notice small diamonds between the knots after you finish the tying. (See figure 41). If, after tying a knot, you cannot see this diamond shape, it probably means that you have taken the wrong strings, and you should untie the knot and check to see that you have not omitted a string or made some other mistake.

NOTE: When making a belt or any other long project, you will have to reposition your work on the wood base after you have knotted two or three inches. To do this, take the knotted macramé off the nails on which it is anchored, and move your

23

work back; then reset the new work again on the piece of backing wood. Nail the macramé again—this time through the knots. Moving the work back makes knotting the macramé easier and the knots more secure.

Even if your strings are very long, you should always leave them hanging loose while you are working. Select the strings you want to work with as you need them.

WORKING FROM A BUCKLE

If you are working directly on a buckle, loop your double strings directly on your buckle, as you did on the short working string, A–B (fig. 29). However, you have to make sure that the number of strings you have is evenly divisible by four. You can work with eight, twelve, sixteen, twenty-four, or even more strings. After you have the desired number of strings evenly attached to your buckle—the same number on each side of the prong—proceed as described on page 17 and 18. Notice how the strings are attached to the buckle in figure 42.

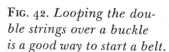

FIG. 42. *Looping the double strings over a buckle is a good way to start a belt.*

3

ANOTHER
METHOD AND
OTHER KNOTS

THIS chapter introduces an alternate method of tying the Square Knot: tying the knot in two parts. Half Knots are used in making spiral shapes, and instruction for making twisted knots are given in this chapter. The Half Hitch and the Wing Knot are also described, and the chapter closes with directions for joining string.

THE SECOND METHOD OF TYING
A SQUARE KNOT—PART ONE

Since you have mastered the Square Knot using one method, you should learn how to make a Square Knot another way, using a second method. You need to know the second method for two reasons. First, when your string is getting quite short, near the end of a belt, you will have to use this method. Second, you need to learn this other method if you want to master the twisted technique, or as some people call it, the Spiral.

As you know, the Square Knot is made with two tying steps. The first step is making the loops and the second is adjusting the two knots to complete the one Square Knot. Now let's learn how to make the Square Knot by tying two Half Knots. As before, you still need four ends of string to make a Square

FIG. 43. *Belts showing many knots in process.*

2 5

Knot, so take the first four strings, select the two middle ones (strings 2 and 3) and attach these two strings to your waist string or waist hook.

Now take the left-hand string (string 1) with your left hand, hold it with your finger on the left side of the center strings. With your right hand, pass the end across and under the two center strings toward the right. Next, take the right-hand string (string 4), bring it underneath string 1, then across and over the two center strings (going toward the left), then down inside the loop between strings 1 and 2 and pull it tight (fig. 44). You have completed part one of the two-part Square Knot.

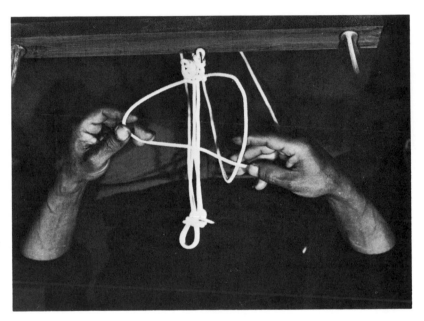

FIG. 44. *String 1 goes across and under the two center strings.*

PART TWO OF A TWO-PART SQUARE KNOT

As you can see, string 1 is now on the right side, and string 4 is on the left. To do the other part of the knot, you must bring strings 1 and 4 back to their original positions. So, for the second part of the knot, you must hold string 4 (which is now in the number 1 string position on the left side) with the left finger, and with the right hand, bring the end over across the two middle strings to the right side. Next, take the right-hand string (or former number 1 string) over former string 4, down and across and underneath the two middle strings and up in the hole between the strings 4 and 2 and tie it tight. This is the second part of the knot, and you will now see that your Square Knot is done. (See figures 45–50 for the second part of the knot.)

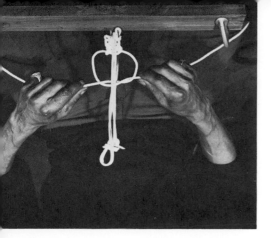

FIG. 45. *String 4 goes under string 1, then across and over the two center strings.*

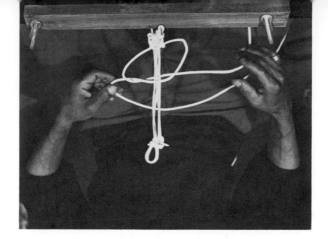

FIG. 46. *The first part of the two-part method of tying a Square Knot.*

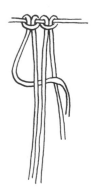

A

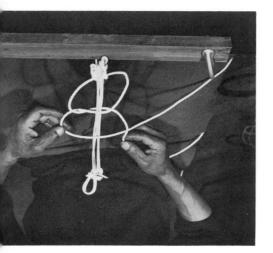

FIG. 47. *Starting the second part of the two-part knot.*

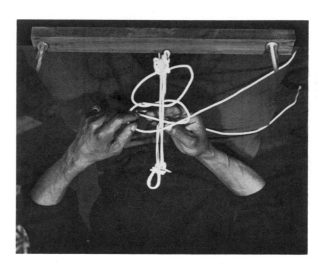

FIG. 48. *Tying the second part of the knot.*

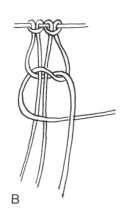

B

C

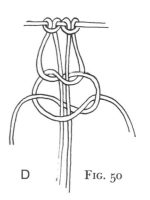

FIG. 49. *Tie each knot tightly.*

D   FIG. 50

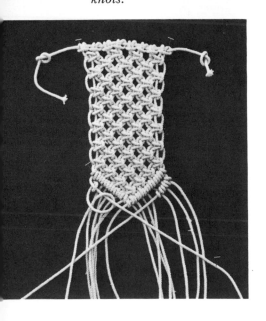

MAKING A TWISTED SENNIT WITH A SPIRAL KNOT

To make the twisted sennit or Spiral, you need the usual four ends of string. Attach the middle strings (2 and 3) to your waist string, then take the left-hand string 1 with your left hand. Hold string 1 on the left side of the center strings. With the right hand, pass the end across and under the center strings to the right. Next, take the right-hand string (string 4) underneath string 1, then over across the center strings and down inside the loop between strings 1 and 2 and tie it tight. In other words, you repeat the first half of the second method for tying a Square Knot over and over again, and it will form a Spiral as you go (fig. 51). Using the procedure just described, the sennit will twist to the left. If you want the twist to go to the right, you must use the second part of the knot rather than the first.

FIG. 51. *A sennit of twisted knots.*

OTHER USES OF THE DOUBLE HALF HITCH

This is a very useful knot, because it can be used for many different purposes. It can be knotted horizontally, vertically, or diagonally, but is most effective when it is horizontal or diagonal. You have already used this knot (p. 20) to finish your first belt. It is a particularly suitable way to finish work, because it provides a firm, strong line. It can also be used as an integral part of a design. For example, it may be used inside or outside an inverted V made in a floating string design, as shown on p. 41 and on page 73 in figure 107.

If different colors are used when you are making Double Half Hitches, the color changes as the string is moved across the piece, and this can be very effective.

If it is necessary to take the knot-bearing string back to its original position, another row of Double Half Hitches must be made over this string.

It is possible to produce a piece of work made entirely of Double Half Hitches, but this takes a very long time and is not recommended for the beginner.

Exact instructions for making the Double Half Hitch are given on pages 20 and 21.

FIG. 52. *Double Half Hitches used to finish a belt.*

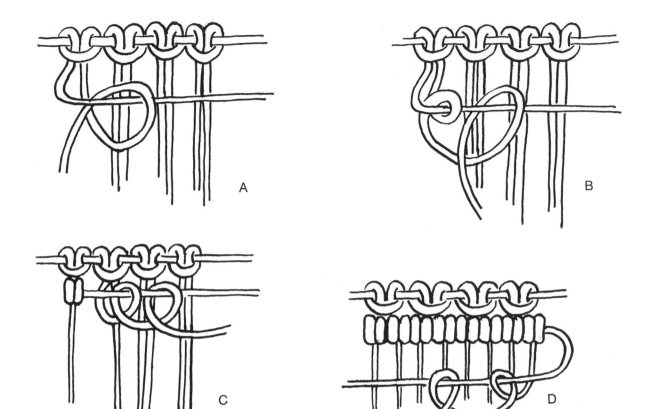

FIG. 53

WING KNOTS

A Wing Knot is a Square Knot with a loop on each side. This loop gives the appearance of little wings, and from this comes the name. Like other Square Knots, it is made with four strings, and it is extremely easy to make. Used correctly, this knot can be very effective. In order to make Wing Knots you must make a series of knots with four strings. However, you must make your knots about one inch apart. Then, after tying each knot, you must move the knot up on the string, and push it as close to the preceding knot as possible. By doing this, a loop is formed on each side of the knot, like two little wings.

FIG. 54

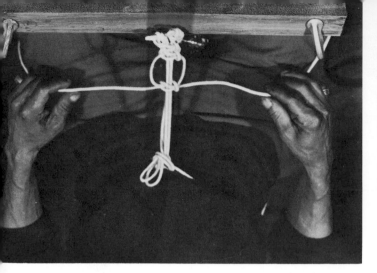

FIG. 55. *Starting a Wing Knot.*

FIG. 56. *Pushing the Wing Knot up on the middle strings so that the little "wings" show.*

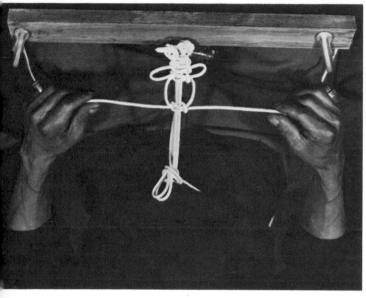

FIG. 57. *Positioning the knot.*

FIG. 58. *The second Wing Knot.*

FIG. 59. *A series of Wing Knots.*

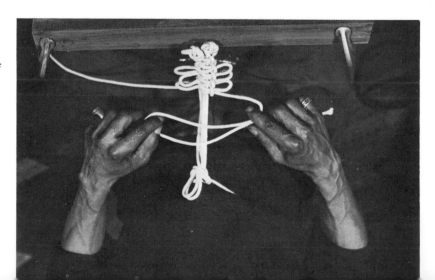

3 0

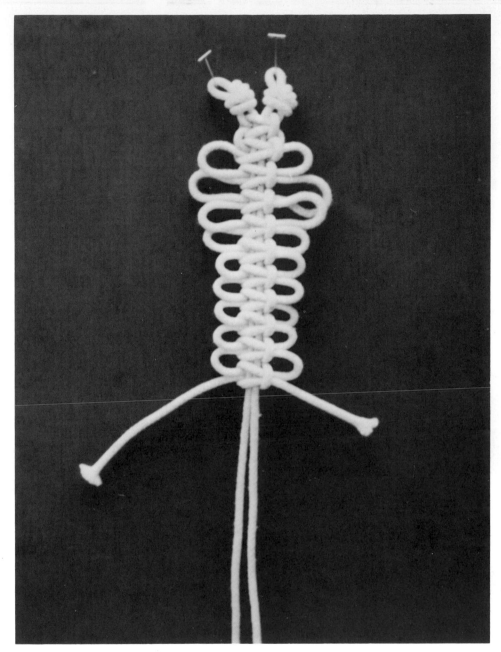

FIG. 60. *A sennit of Wing Knots.*

SPACE KNOTS

The Space Knot is a variation of the Wing Knot. Instead of pushing the knots close together, as you do when you make a wing knot, this time you do not move the knot to be near the preceding one. Instead, you leave them with a space of about one-half inch between the knots. This gives a slightly lacy effect to the sides of the sennit.

3 1

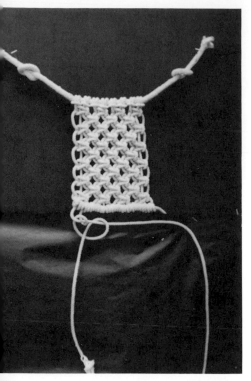

FIG. 61. *Horizontal Double Half Hitch.*

LOOSE KNOTS

Loose Knots are frequently used on wall hangings, and they are very decorative. They are quite similar to standard Square Knots, but they are made with a space of one-half inch or one inch between the rows. These knots are very attractive when they are used in combination with weaving, as described and shown in the illustrations for chapter 8 (p. 103, figs. 134 and 136).

HORIZONTAL DOUBLE HALF HITCH

When making horizontal Double Half Hitches, you take the string on the left as a filler and make two Half Hitches on top of it with all the other strings, one after another, until you reach the last string. Start by taking string 1 with the right hand. Hold string 2 with the index finger of the right hand on the right side of string 1, then pass it underneath string 1, over it, then down through the loop between strings 1 and 2 and pull tight. Make another Half Hitch in the same way, with the same string. Then take the next string, string 3, while still holding string 1 as you did before; pass it underneath string 1, over it and down inside the loop between strings 3 and 1. Continue in this way until string 1 reaches the end.

DIAGONAL DOUBLE HALF HITCH

If your work is already shaped diagonally, proceed as you did for the horizontal Double Half Hitch, following the angle of your work. If your work is not already in a diagonal shape, and you wish to make diagonal Double Half Hitches, you have to hold string 1 in such a way that it moves from left to right in a diagonal direction while you are tying the Double Half Hitches. Some people find it easier to secure the first Half Hitch with a pin, while tying the second one.

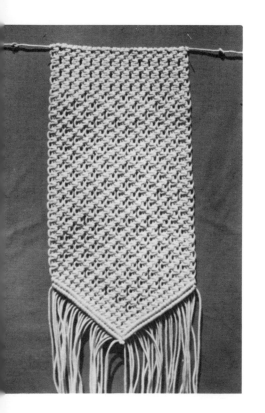

FIG. 62. *A diagonal Double Half Hitch is used to finish a handbag.*

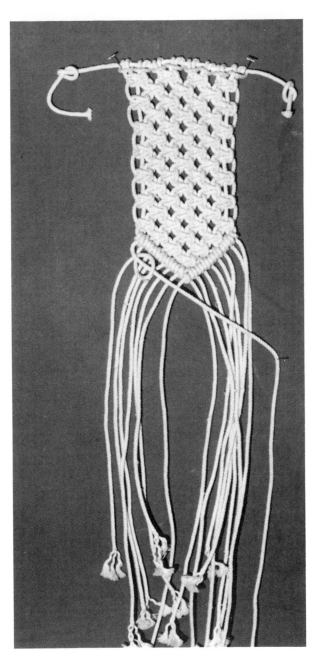

FIG. 63. *The diagonal Double Half Hitch.*

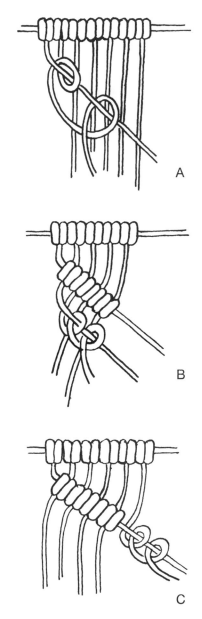

FIG. 64. *Diagonal Double Half Hitch.*

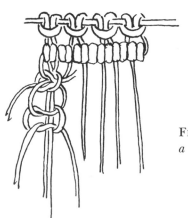

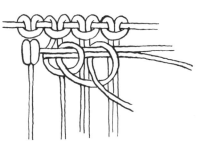

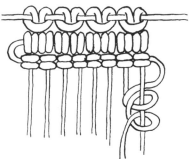

VERTICAL DOUBLE HALF HITCHES

The first string, string 1, is used to make two Half Hitches on top of each string, working across all the strings until you reach the other side of the work. If you start on the left, hold string 1 with the right hand and string 2 with the left hand on top of string 1. Hold string 1 with two fingers on the right of string 2, while the end of string 1 goes over string 2, then underneath and in the loop between strings 1 and 2. Pull tight, then repeat once more. For the next step, do the same thing with strings 1 and 3.

FIG. 66. *Vertical and horizontal Double Half Hitches.*

FIG. 65. *Square Knots followed by a series of vertical Half Hitches.*

JOINING STRINGS

Sometimes you must add a string because your strings have become too short, or one string is shorter than the others. Whenever you do have to add string, it should be done with great care so that the joint is as nearly invisible as possible. Carry the old string along with the new string for a short distance—about two inches. Then, in the second half of the Square Knot, if you use a two-part knot, use both the old and the new string for tying the knot.

Figure 67 shows a new string being added to a Square Knot. This new string will then be used to tie another knot. A new string can also be added to the knot-bearing string when doing horizontal Double Half Hitches. When you do this, let the two strings run parallel and the several Double Half Hitches over both strings until the new string is secure (fig. 68). New strings are added in similar fashion to the knot-bearing string in vertical and diagonal Double Half Hitches.

FIG. 67. *Joining string for a Double Half Hitch.*

FIG. 68. *Joining string for a Square Knot.*

4

FIRST DESIGNS

FIG. 69. *The texture of a variety of knots makes these headbands look more complicated than they are.*

NOW that you have learned the basic knots of macramé, as described in chapter 2, "Tying the Basic Knot," and chapter 3, "Another Method and Other Knots," you can use these knots to make macramé designs.

Square Knots can be worked in many ways. They can be worked horizontally—as in the first belt you made, described on page 15—and also vertically or diagonally. You should experiment with all of the knots you know and create your own designs. This chapter will provide some suggestions for the various possibilities that might be explored. The projects that are described are closely knotted belts, only because belts offer the best method for learning new knots and variations of knots you already know. The first belt in this chapter consists of knots made vertically in groups of two, alternating with horizontal rows of Square Knots.

The main step to be mastered in this chapter is floating string design. In floating string design, spaces are left so that straight strings are surrounded by Square Knots. The most effective designs are of diamond-shaped spaces bounded by diagonal lines of Square Knots. Such designs are known as inside floating string patterns.

Another kind of design is the outside floating string design. In this design there are loose straight strings on the outside of the work that surround solid shapes of knots in the center of the work.

FIG. 70. *Floating string designs can be used in small pieces or large wall hangings.*

In this chapter, the floating string designs are all small in scale, because they are the easiest to learn. However, these ideas can later be interpreted for use in very large pieces. Great care should be taken to keep all the knots as even and symmetrical as possible while you work. The knots should also be tightly tied, even if a space is being left. To make even, tight, and symmetrical knots, considerable practice is necessary.

It will probably be necessary to undertake several projects before you completely master the technique of floating string designs and they are no longer difficult. The way is then open for you to begin to use macramé as an art form—for experiments in line and space, and in your own designs for wall hangings.

Although wall hangings sometimes consist of closely knotted and complicated designs, by a glance at photographs of hangings, or by studying the hangings themselves, you will see that most wall hangings are an elaboration of floating string designs.

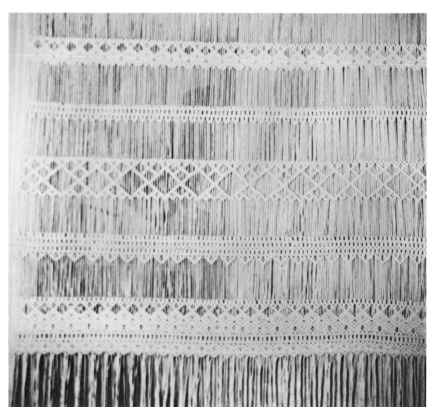

FIG. 71. *A sample of floating string designs.*

FIG. 72. *The fourth row of Belt Two has only three knots.*

You have already made one Square Knot belt, so this will be your second style of belt. For this belt, it is best if you use the same number of strings as you did for the other one—16 string ends (see p. 15). There should be 8 double strings to make the 16 ends. Proceed as you did for the first and second rows in your first belt—four knots for the first row; three knots for the second. However, instead of making one knot, you may make a row of double knots (see figure 71 for a close-up view). The fourth row is single knots and the fifth row double knots (see figure 72). Proceed in this way until your work is of the required length. Your last row will consist of single knots, as on the first belt. The next step is to shape your work to a point as described on pages 19 and 20, and then to finish the belt with Double Half Hitches as you did for your first belt. Figure 73 shows this completed project.

You can consider this design a combination of two knots interlocked with one knot, or two and one. You can also make variations, for instance, two and two, or three and two, or one and three, and so forth.

NOTE: Do not forget to move your work back on the wooden board every time you have knotted about two or three inches of your design. Moving the work back will give support to the knotting and make your work easier.

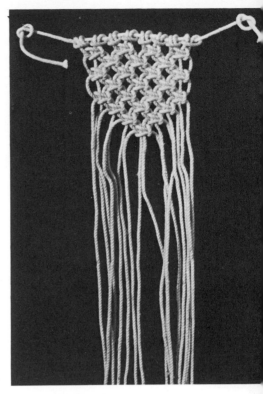

FIG. 73. *Row 5 has four knots; row 6, three knots; row 7, two knots; and row 8, only one knot.*

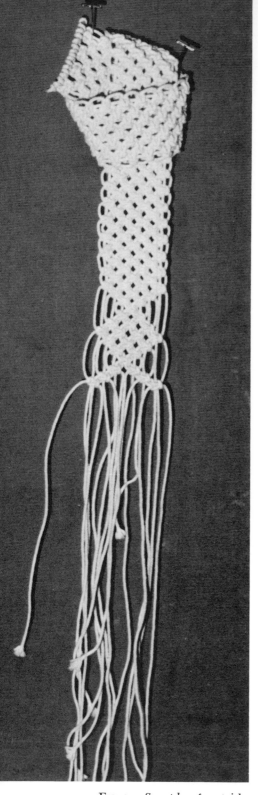

FIG. 74. *Sample of outside floating string.*

To make this belt, we will continue with the same number of strings, so that these trial pieces or sample belts will be simple and the designs easy to follow.

Take 8 double strings, or 16 ends. Begin as you did for your second belt. After you have knotted about two or four rows of macramé knots, you must start to shape the knots to a point as you have done before in finishing a belt (fig. 34). Next, imagine that you are dividing your work into two parts, 8 strings in the right section and 8 strings in the left section. You are going to work left from the center to the left-hand edge and then right from the center to the right-hand edge. These knots must be tied in such a way that when both sides are completed, there will be an inverted V shape, of macramé knots, that is surrounded by floating strings.

Great care should be taken when tying the macramé knots to tie them parallel to each other. When first working with floating string designs, there is a tendency to tie the knots sideways, and this should be avoided.

Now let us start from the left. Select strings number 5, 6, 7, and 8, and counting from the left, attach strings 6 and 7 to the waist string or waist hook and make a Square Knot in the usual way. Then take strings number 3, 4, 5, and 6 and attach strings 4 and 5 to your waist and tie a knot with strings 6 and 3. Next, select strings number 1, 2, 3, and 4 and attach strings 2 and 3 to your waist and make a knot with strings 4 and 1. This will be the last knot on the left side of the floating string design.

Now go to the right-hand side and proceed to select and use strings 9, 10, 11, and 12. Attach strings 10 and 11 to your waist and tie a Square Knot with strings 12 and 9. This knot must be on the same level as the first knot on the left and, of course, parallel to the other knots. Then take strings 11, 12, 13, and 14; take 12 and 13 for your middle string and tie a knot with strings 14 and 11. The next knot will be made with strings 13, 14, 15, and 16. Select the middle strings, 14 and 15, and tie a knot with 16 and 13.

When you have finished the last knot on the right, you will notice an empty space in the middle, shaped like a forty-five-degree angle. You can now fill this space with a few knots, and at the same time, you can shape your knots to a point again, so that your design can be repeated.

To fill up the middle or empty space, select strings 7, 8, 9, and 10; take 8 and 9 for your waist strings and tie a knot with strings 10 and 7. The next knot will be tied with strings 5, 6, 7, and 8. Then take strings 9, 10, 11, and 12; tie your knot, and you will notice a straight horizontal row of knots.

You are now ready to start the pointed shape. Select strings 3, 4, 5, and 6 and tie a Square Knot. Then take strings 7, 8, 9, and 10 and tie a knot; select strings 11, 12, 13, and 14 and tie a knot. You are now ready for another row. Take strings 5, 6, 7, and 8 and tie a knot. Next, select strings 9, 10, 11, and 12 and tie a knot. The last knot to finish the pointed shape will be made from strings 7, 8, 9, and 10. If you continue to repeat your design in the same way you will make an interesting and attractive belt (see figure 75).

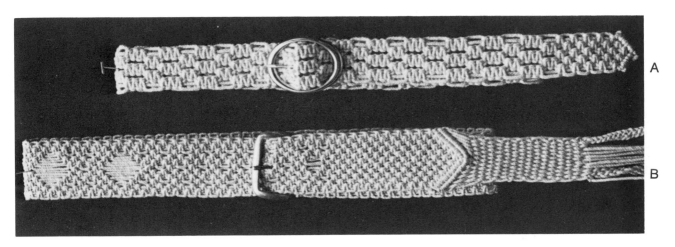

Inside Floating String—Belt Four

When making an inside floating string design for a belt or for any other piece of work, you must first build the left corner to a pointed shape and then build the right corner to a pointed shape, so that an empty space of floating strings is framed by the macramé knots. Work with the same number of strings that you have been working with—16 ends made from 8 double strings. This will make four Square Knots. I would not advise anyone to start the floating string design on the first row of knots, unless you have considerable experience and a great deal of confidence. You should start the inside floating string design on the third row of knots, so that you have four knots to work from. (Row 2 has only three knots across.)

In this belt the design is symmetrical and goes in a diagonal direction, so that you have an empty space inside a diamond-shaped frame. Like the outside floating string design, the inside

FIG. 75. *A: Belt showing double-knot combinations; B: Belt showing large and small inside floating string design combined with single knot.*

39

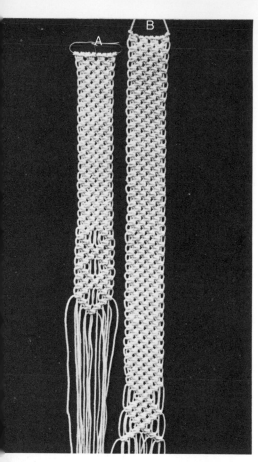

FIG. 76. *A: Inside floating string design; B: Outside floating string design.*

FIG. 77. *Row of single knots combined with double knots starting from buckle.*

design is made in two parts—the left side and the right side. After working each of the two sides separately and diagonally, you will join both together at the end of the finished design (see figure 76).

You are now ready to try the inside floating string design. Start on the left. Select strings number 3, 4, 5, and 6; tie a Square Knot with these ends. Do not forget, all knots must be parallel to each other. Now take strings number 5, 6, 7, and 8 and tie a knot. This constitutes one half of the left half of your floating string design.

The next step is to go to the right side of the design. Select strings 11, 12, 13, and 14 and tie a knot. Then select strings 9, 10, 11, and 12 and do the same knotting with this end as you did on the other side (the left side) of your design. You must now join both sides together. Select strings 7, 8, 9, and 10 and tie a knot. This last Square Knot will end your inside floating string design (see figure 76).

You can combine both the outside and the inside floating string designs if you want that kind of effect. (See figure 78). If you want to use only the inside string to float, you must fill up both sides and shape your work to a V once again, and then repeat the design.

Belt with Loop and Buckle—Belt Five

When starting a belt with a loop to which the buckle is attached, the following procedure is suggested. If you have a buckle you want to use, you must plan exactly how wide your belt is going to be, since you must know how many strings you will need to fit on this buckle. When you calculate the number of strings needed to fit your buckle, be sure to remember that the number must always be divisible by four. Sixteen, twenty, twenty-four, or twenty-eight strings (for a very wide belt) will work very well.

To start, measure out twine equal to $7\frac{1}{2}$ or 8 times the required length of your belt. You will begin working from the middle of these strings. For example, if your belt is to be one yard in length, you will need 8 yards of twine. Start in the middle—that is 4 yards from the end—and make the first row of Square Knots and the second row. Continue knotting but shape your work diagonally so that there is a point on the left-hand side. Then turn your work over and shape the other side in the same way to a diagonal shape pointing to the left. In this way, both long edges will be on the same side. For instance, if you are making a belt with 24 strings, or 6 Square Knots per row, when you start in the middle you only work with three Square Knots. These three knots are half of the width of the belt. The longer edge should be 2⅓ times the width of your belt.

Next, you must fold your work and bring the two pointed edges close together to form the loop and pin or nail it to the working place. Make the joined knot by taking two strings on each side of the pointed edge. Then use the second string on each pointed edge for the middle, or filler, and the first string on each side for tying the knot. Continue knotting by taking two strings from the first knot and two strings from the side until you fill up the empty space. Then continue working up to the desired length, or until the belt is finished.

COLORED BELTS

The other belts in this chapter are all made of colored nylon cord. This cord is much thicker than string, so that the technique of working with it is different from the technique of working with string. Nylon cord is slippery to knot, but it has the advantage of being much quicker to work with than the twine. However, this is only because it is so thick.

The bright colors also allow completely different effects than those possible with simple string. Do not try to use a buckle with this cord. It is too thick, and it would be very clumsy.

The following are descriptions of how some of the belts that are pictured in figure 78 can be made.

The gold belt is made with an outside and inside floating string design combined with diagonal Half Hitches forming diamond shapes. The ends are finished with two rows of Double Half Hitches. The four center cords are left long to tie.

The two-color belt is made of blue and red cord. There are four blue cords in the center and four red on each side; the design is inside and outside floating string.

The three-color belt is made of green, orange, and gold cord, arranged as follows: four gold, four green, four orange, and four gold. As in the other belts, the design is worked in inside and outside floating string design combined with Half Hitches. This is a wide belt of 16 string ends. All of the ends have been left loose, and the belt is tied around the waist, using the string ends.

FIG. 78.
Examples of colored belts.

I have used nylon cord and worked all the projects in colored string. However, the colors I've used are not the ones you might want. I've left references to color in the text because it is often easier to follow color references, and the use of the color acts as a double check on whether you are working with the correct string. You may want to make a chart for each of the projects. You can adapt my directions on your chart, using the colors of your choice.

5

SOME PRACTICAL USES FOR MACRAMÉ

BELTS are not only attractive and useful projects for macramé, but they also serve as an excellent way to learn this craft. If you have mastered the basic techniques of knotting by making the belts described in chapters 2, 3, and 4, you are now ready to progress further and to work on some more challenging designs. In this chapter, we suggest some of the practical uses for macramé and some ideas for other projects in which this craft can be used.

The first practical projects will be a handbag, and a shopping bag. The student of macramé can adapt the directions that are given if he would like to experiment, and once he has some experience in knotting these projects, he can continue on his own. This chapter also provides instructions for two necklaces, a headband, and a choker. Lastly, there is a description of how to make two different styles of skirts.

Pocketbook or Handbag

Since you have practiced and mastered the basic knotting techniques, you are now going to make a small handbag. This

FIG. 79. *This handbag, made of lilac-colored cord, was made in Rimini, Italy. It is made of diagonal Double Half Hitches combined with single knots. The bag is lined and has a zipper closure.*

bag is made with fourteen Square Knots which means you will need 28 double strings and 56 ends.

First, measure your double strings—all 28 of them; each double string should be 60 inches long. Loop all of the double strings on a work string that is about 25 inches long.

Nail your work string onto a piece of wood that is about 2 inches wide and at least 15 inches long. Clamp the piece of wood to the end of the table where you are going to work.

The first row of Square Knots should be made starting with strings number 1, 2, 3, and 4 and knotted so that you have fourteen knots. For the second row, join the first knot to the second, the second to the third, the third to the fourth and so on, until you finish the second row with thirteen knots. On the third row, you are going to start the first design as shown in figure 72, so that the third row will be double knots and the fourth row will be single knots.

However, before you start the double knots on the third row, there is one bit of advice I would like to give you. Take an object with a straight edge, or a ruler, and make a pencil line about a quarter of an inch away from the near edge of the piece of wood that you use for supporting the work. Then, nail your work on top of that straight pencil line. Keeping your work

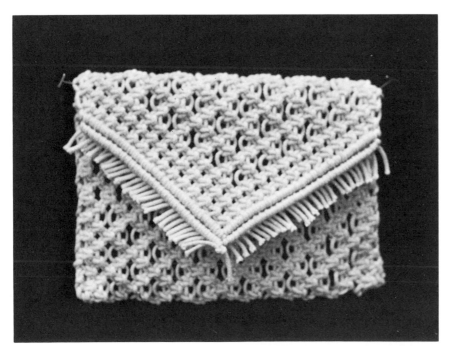

FIG. 80. *A macramé bag is especially nice for summer use. This bag can be used in the basic envelope style, or a sennit can be added to make it a shoulder bag. If you prefer a large bag, or one with many compartments, two of these bags can be made, and sewn back-to-back.*

even with the pencil line on the wood will help to make your bag look professional and neat. Also, remember to move—be sure you are always positioned in front of the knot you are tying. If you are not, it is easy to become confused or to absent-mindedly pick up the wrong string. After you have drawn the working pencil line and checked your position in front of the knotting, you are ready to make the third row of double knots.

Let us review the work:

Row 3 is double knots
Row 4 is single knots
Row 5 is double knots
Row 6 is single knots
Row 7 is double knots
Row 8 is single knots

Do not forget that after you have knotted about one inch, you must move your work back, so that the row you are knotting is over the pencil line guide.

After you have finished row 8—a row of single knots— you are going to change the design to make an inside floating string design as shown in the sample (fig. 76–A). In the left-hand corner, tie the first knot for this design. Use strings 1, 2, 3, and 4, counting from left to right. Leave the second group of knot strings untied, then tie the third knot with strings 9, 10, 11, and 12. Skip the next group of four strings and tie a knot with strings 17, 18, 19, and 20. Continue as follows:

Tie strings 25, 26, 27, 28.
Tie strings 33, 34, 35, 36.
Tie strings 41, 42, 43, 44.
Tie strings 49, 50, 51, 52.
Tie strings 53, 54, 55, 56.

You will notice that the design stops with strings 49, 50, 51, and 52. It will continue later on. You have now begun to build the point shape.

Most of these designs are symmetrical or diagonal. Do not forget that the floating string design is made of two parts, no matter how large it is: the left side and the right side. After working on each side separately, you then join the end of both sides together. I am going to give you a step-by-step explanation of how to proceed in the easiest way possible.

Row 1 of Floating String

Go to the left-hand side and, counting from left to right, take strings 3, 4, 5, and 6 and tie a knot. Next, tie strings 7, 8, 9, 10.

Then take strings 5, 6, 7, and 8 and tie a knot. You will see that this third knot joins the first two together so that they form a small diamond shape (see figure 81). Continue working knots in groups of three across the row as follows:

Tie strings 11, 12, 13, 14.
Tie strings 15, 16, 17, 18.
Then join them with a knot tied with strings 13, 14, 15, 16.
Tie strings 19, 20, 21, 22.
Tie strings 23, 24, 25, 26.
Join them with a knot tied with strings 21, 22, 23, 24.
Tie strings 27, 28, 29, 30.
Tie strings 31, 32, 33, 34.
Join them with a knot tied with strings 29, 30, 31, 32.
Tie strings 35, 36, 37, 38.
Tie strings 39, 40, 41, 42.
Join them with a knot tied with strings 37, 38, 39, 40.
Tie strings 43, 44, 45, 46.
Tie strings 47, 48, 49, 50.
Join them with a knot tied with strings 45, 46, 47, 48.
Tie strings 51, 52, 53, 54.
Tie strings 53, 54, 55, 56 to finish the first row.

You are now ready to repeat your design. This will be the second row of your inside floating string design. I suggest that you again go back to the left-hand corner.

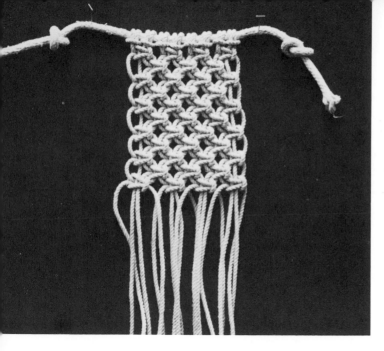

FIG. 81. *Notice the small diamond shape between the knots.*

Row 2 of Inside Floating String

Tie strings 1, 2, 3, 4.
Tie strings 7, 8, 9, 10.
Tie strings 11, 12, 13, 14.
To join them, tie strings 9, 10, 11, 12.
Tie strings 15, 16, 17, 18.
Tie strings 19, 20, 21, 22.
To join them, tie strings 17, 18, 19, 20.
Tie strings 23, 24, 25, 26.
Tie strings 27, 28, 29, 30.
To join them, tie strings 25, 26, 27, 28.
Tie strings 31, 32, 33, 34.
Tie strings 35, 36, 37, 38.
To join them, tie strings 33, 34, 35, 36.
Tie strings 39, 40, 41, 42.
Tie strings 43, 44, 45, 46.
To join them, tie strings 41, 42, 43, 44.
Tie strings 47, 48, 49, 50.
Tie strings 51, 52, 53, 54.
To join them, tie strings 49, 50, 51, 52.
Tie strings 53, 54, 55, 56.

47

Go back to the left-hand side to build it up in preparation for the third row.

Tie strings 3, 4, 5, 6.
Tie strings 1, 2, 3, 4.

This will be the end of the second row of inside floating string. The design also prepares for the third row.

The knots used on the first and second rows, as already described, form the pattern and are repeated until a total of 20 rows have been worked. Your work will then be approximately 12 inches in length. Do not forget that as you work you must move your knotting back each time after you have knotted one inch.

Row 21 of Floating String

For this row you are going to shape it to a point, so you don't start at the corner as for the other rows. Go back to the left-hand side and, counting from left to right, take strings 11, 12, 13, and 14 and tie a knot.

Tie strings 15, 16, 17, 18.
Join them with a knot tied with strings 13, 14, 15, 16.
Tie strings 19, 20, 21, 22.
Tie strings 23, 24, 25, 26.
Join them with a knot tied with strings 21, 22, 23, 24.
Tie strings 27, 28, 29, 30.
Tie strings 31, 32, 33, 34.
Join them with a knot tied with strings 29, 30, 31, 32.
Tie strings 35, 36, 37, 38.
Tie strings 39, 40, 41, 42.
Join them with a knot tied with strings 37, 38, 39, 40.
Tie strings 43, 44, 45, 46.
Tie strings 47, 48, 49, 50.
Join them with a knot tied with strings 45, 46, 47, 48.
Tie strings 51, 52, 53, 54.
Go back to the left-hand side.
Tie strings 3, 4, 5, 6.
Tie strings 1, 2, 3, 4.

Plate 1. Myriam Gilby, *Rhythm of Blue Verticals*. 60 inches by 52 inches; cotton warp. Mainly tapestry techniques with manipulated hanging warps, metal industrial waste, and some macramé.

Plate 2. Myriam Gilby.
Tassel Doll Hanging.
50 inches by 30 inches;
Tapestry and macramé combined.

Plate 3. Mary A. Auty. *Lion.*
53 inches by 40 inches;
cotton and wool. Tapestry and
hooking combined.

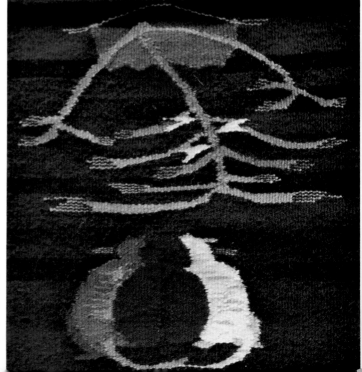

Plate 4. Bewick-Ball.
September Sunset.
Wall hanging using weaving,
crochet, and macramé. All handspun
wool was used in order to provide
a variety of textures.

Plate 5. Arlene Kukafka.
Our Three Cats.
14 inches by 16 inches.
Interlocking and dovetailing tapestry
techniques were used.
Photograph by Karen Goldstein.

Plate 6. J. A. Halder.
High Up, Far North.
Linen warp, plain weaving
with unspun plant-dyed woo

Plate 7. Spencer Dépas.
Three macramé headbands
worked in nylon cord.

Plate 8. Spencer Dépas. *The Drummer.* 36 inches by 63 inches.

Plate 9. Lili Blumenau. Tapestry on white background. **Plate 10.** Lili Blumenau. *Woman with Baskets.*

Plate 11. Spencer Dépas. Macramé worked in nylon; floating string gives a feeling of openwork.

Plate 12. Myriam Gilby. *Growth*. 84 inches by 58 inches. This hanging was first shown at the Scottish Arts Council's exhibition. The warp is horsehair, the weft horsehair, bean strings, jute, metal industrial waste, metal washers, curtain wire, rags, and string. Some macramé techniques were used in the weft as well as in the hanging's warp.

Tie strings 5, 6, 7, 8.
Tie strings 7, 8, 9, 10.
Tie strings 3, 4, 5, 6.
You are now prepared for Row 22.

Row 22 of Floating String

Tie strings 15, 16, 17, 18.
Tie strings 19, 20, 21, 22.
Join them with a knot tied with strings 17, 18, 19, 20.
Tie strings 23, 24, 25, 26.
Tie strings 27, 28, 29, 30.
Join them with a knot tied with strings 25, 26, 27, 28.
Tie strings 31, 32, 33, 34.
Tie strings 35, 36, 37, 38.
Join them with a knot tied with strings 33, 34, 35, 36.
Tie strings 39, 40, 41, 42.
Tie strings 43, 44, 45, 46.
Join them with a knot tied with strings 41, 42, 43, 44.
Tie strings 49, 50, 51, 52.
Tie strings 47, 48, 49, 50.
Tie strings 45, 46, 47, 48.
Go back to the left-hand side.

Row 23 of Floating String

Tie strings 9, 10, 11, 12.
Tie strings 11, 12, 13, 14.
Tie strings 13, 14, 15, 16.
Tie strings 19, 20, 21, 22.
Tie strings 23, 24, 25, 26.
Join them with a knot tied with strings 21, 22, 23, 24.
Tie strings 27, 28, 29, 30.
Tie strings 31, 32, 33, 34.
Join them with a knot tied with strings 29, 30, 31, 32.
Tie strings 35, 36, 37, 38.
Tie strings 39, 40, 41, 42.
Join them with a knot tied with strings 37, 38, 39, 40.
Tie strings 43, 44, 45, 46.
Tie strings 41, 42, 43, 44.

Go back to the left-hand side.
Tie strings 5, 6, 7, 8.
Tie strings 7, 8, 9, 10.
Tie strings 9, 10, 11, 12.
Tie strings 15, 16, 17, 18.
Tie strings 17, 18, 19, 20.
Tie strings 23, 24, 25, 26.
Tie strings 27, 28, 29, 30.
To join them, tie strings 25, 26, 27, 28.
Tie strings 31, 32, 33, 34.
Tie strings 35, 36, 37, 38.
To join them, tie strings 33, 34, 35, 36.
Tie strings 27, 28, 29, 30.
Tie strings 31, 32, 33, 34.
To join them, tie strings 29, 30, 31, 32.
Tie strings 39, 40, 41, 42.
Tie strings 37, 38, 39, 40.
Tie strings 35, 36, 37, 38.
Tie strings 33, 34, 35, 36.
Tie strings 31, 32, 33, 34.
Go back to the left-hand side.
Tie strings 19, 20, 21, 22.
Tie strings 21, 22, 23, 24.
Tie strings 23, 24, 25, 26.
Tie strings 25, 26, 27, 28.
Tie strings 27, 28, 29, 30.
Tie strings 29, 30, 31, 32.
Go back to the left-hand side.
Tie strings 11, 12, 13, 14.
Tie strings 13, 14, 15, 16.
Tie strings 15, 16, 17, 18.
Tie strings 17, 18, 19, 20.
Tie strings 19, 20, 21, 22.
Tie strings 21, 22, 23, 24.
Tie strings 23, 24, 25, 26.
Tie strings 25, 26, 27, 28.
Tie strings 27, 28, 29, 30.
This is the last knot to do.

FINISHING THE HANDBAG

The finishing is with a Double Half Hitch, just like the finishing of the belt in chapter 2, pages 19–21.

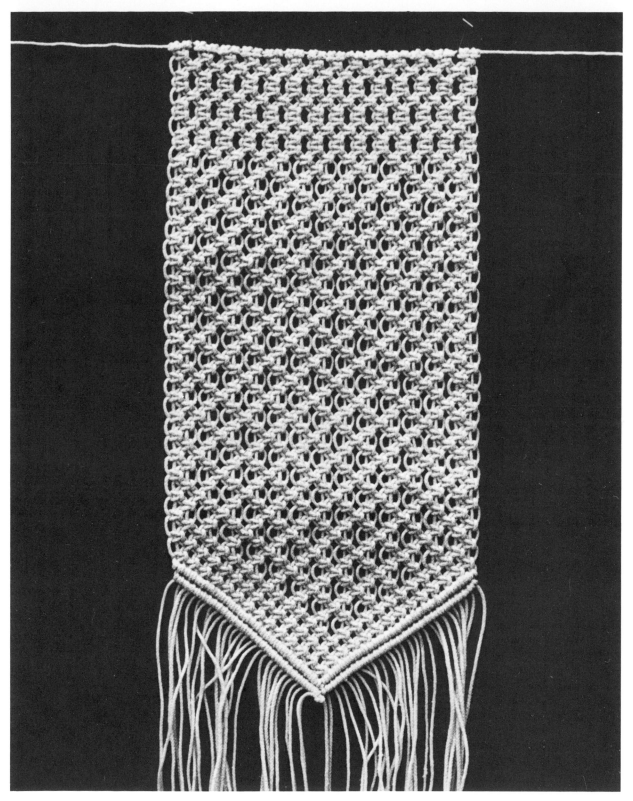

FIG. 82. *Tie each knot carefully so that the finished bag has even knots and straight edges.*

Take the first string on the left and make it go diagonally to the center by making a Double Half Hitch knot on top of it with each string on the left-hand side, until it reaches the center of your work.

Then, go to the right-hand side, take the last string (string 56) and do the same thing, going in the other direction until the two strings meet at the center. If you wish to have a double row of Half Hitches, repeat the same procedure but always use the last string to cross with on both sides. After that, you can secure the ends by sewing with a needle and thread. You can then cut all extra strings short or leave them in a fringe, or cut them off completely by cutting near the knots.

If you wish to line the handbag, you must do this before folding and sewing the bag. Bags may be lined or left unlined. If you want to leave the macramé bag unlined, just fold it along the line one inch from where the pointed shape starts, and then sew both sides with a needle to form an envelope (see figure 83).

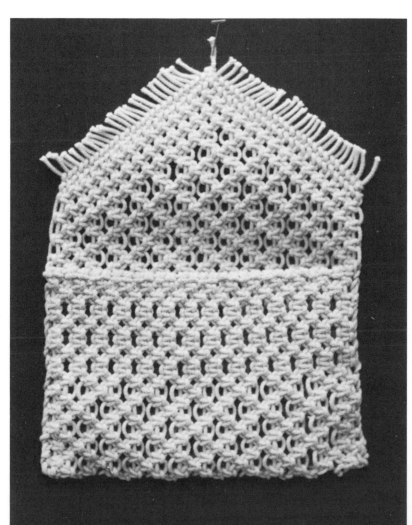

FIG. 83. *An unlined handbag sewn along the edges to form an envelope.*

5 2

If you wish to add a handle to the bag, you can make a separate sennit of macramé, and sew it to the sides and bottom of the bag. You might also want to make a closure for the bag. A large wooden button makes a very nice closure for a macramé bag. If you use a button, be sure that it will not rust or discolor the macramé when the bag is washed.

The last two ends that are left from the Double Half Hitch can be used as a loop to secure the button or other closure.

Macramé bags can also be fitted with zippers. Use a large-toothed zipper and sew the zipper in the pocket of the envelope with small stitches, using a needle and thread.

Shopping Bag

A shopping bag can be made in a number of ways: with regular square knots, loose knots, or floating string designs. The bag described here is very simple, and it is made with an 11-inch wide wooden handle. If you do not have such a handle, you can make this bag on dowel rods, or you can use a wire clothes hanger for a base. The wire must, of course, be covered with macramé knotting, or it will look very odd.

To start, you will need 32 double strings that are each 6 feet long for each side of the handle. That means 64 ends. Each end will be 3 feet long.

Size 30 string or 16-ply wrapping twine can be used.

Loop all the strings over the handle.

Make the first and second row of knots.

Row 3. Make a 3-knot row.

Row 4. Single knots.

Row 5. Make a 3-knot row.

Row 6 and 7. Single knots.

Row 8. Make a horizontal Double Half Hitch row across from left to right.

Row 9. Make a row of single knots.

Row 10. Make another horizontal Double Half Hitch row, but this time work from right to left.

Row 11. Make a row of 4 knots.

Row 12. Make a row of Double Half Hitches.

Row 13. Make a row of 2 knots.

Row 14. Make a row of Double Half Hitches.

FIG. 84. *A shopping bag that could be used as a handbag.*

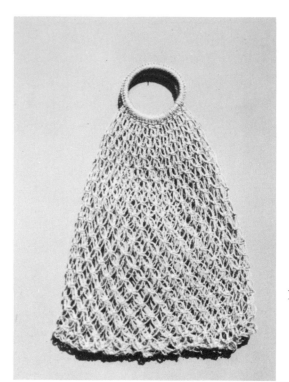

FIG. 85. *An open shopping bag.*

FIG. 86. *A wooden suit hanger, with the wire hook removed, could serve as the handle for this shopping bag. A sennit of cord might be added to make a shoulder bag.*

54

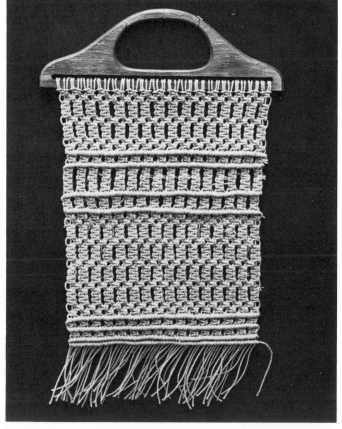

Row 15 and 16. Single knots.

Row 17. Make a row of 3 knots.

Rows 17 to 24. Combine one row of 3 knots with one row single knots.

Row 25. Make a row of single knots.

Row 26. Make a row of Double Half Hitches.

Row 27. Single knots.

Row 28. Make a row of Double Half Hitches.

Row 29. Single knots.

Row 30. To end this side, make a double row of Half Hitches.

Repeat the same on the other side and sew the two sides together.

First Necklace

You can make a necklace of one color or multicolored, with or without beads or with a combination of color and beads. You can loop your double string around a piece of wire or a piece of string that is about 20 inches long. If you use wire, copper wire of about 16 gauge works well. For the average-sized neck, the wire should be about 20 inches long. The ends can be filed smooth with a metal file, or even an emery board, and then twisted to form a hook closure.

The necklace shown is made with cord of three different colors. I've used red, green, and white cord. However, any three colors, or three shades of the same color, can be used. Eight Square Knots or 16 double strings are used. Your double strings should each be 1 yard (36 inches) long and should be looped over the piece of wire. The colors I've used are only suggestions; you can make this necklace in any number and variety of colors.

FIG. 87. *This multicolored macramé piece is being made by looping the double strands over a piece of wire. String can also be used instead of wire. Silver, copper, or brass wire make beautiful bases for macramé. This necklace can be made with or without the beads. Shells, cork, or wood pieces can be used for extra interest. I avoid using glass or ceramic beads, because if the beads break, there is no way to replace them without undoing the entire necklace.*

Knot 1—have 2 double strings, white

Knot 2—have 2 double strings, green

Knot 3—have 2 double strings, white

Knot 4—have 2 double strings, red

Knot 5—have 2 double strings, red

Knot 6—have 2 double strings, white

Knot 7—have 2 double strings, green

Knot 8—have 2 double strings, white

Make the first row of Square Knots, then join the first knot to the second, the second to the third, etc. But before tying the knot, make sure you do not tie it close to the first row. Leave an interval of about ¼ inch before tying each knot.

After the second row of knots, you may place your work on a straight line in order to see what you are making. Then make the third row of knots. After the third row of knots, divide your work into two parts, so that four Square Knots are on the left and four Square Knots are on the right.

Tie strings 11, 12, 13, 14.

Tie strings 7, 8, 9, 10.

Tie strings 3, 4, 5, 6.

Tie strings 1, 2, 3, 4.

Tie strings 5, 6, 7, 8.

Tie strings 9, 10, 11, 12.

Tie strings 3, 4, 5, 6.

Tie strings 7, 8, 9, 10.

Then again tie strings 1, 2, 3, 4.

Tie strings 5, 6, 7, 8.

Tie strings 3, 4, 5, 6.

Tie strings 1, 2, 3, 4.

You now go over to the other half—the right-hand side— still counting from left to right, and tie strings 19, 20, 21, 22.

Tie strings 23, 24, 25, 26.

Tie strings 27, 28, 29, 30.

Tie strings 29, 30, 31, 32.

Tie strings 25, 26, 27, 28.

Tie strings 21, 22, 23, 24.

You continue by knotting strings 23, 24, 25, 26.

Tie strings 27, 28, 29, 30.

Tie strings 29, 30, 31, 32.

Tie strings 25, 26, 27, 28.

Tie strings 27, 28, 29, 30.

Tie strings 29, 30, 31, 32.

After the last knot, take your work off the working table and shape it. It is best to place it around your neck to find out how you are going to shape it into an arc. Then, keeping this shape, nail it again to the worktable. Then take another piece of wire, about 18 inches in length, and shape it into an arc. You are going to join this to your work by knotting Double Half Hitches onto it with each string from 1 to 32. However, before you start, insert the string into the beads where needed. In this necklace, beads are used to form a pattern in the center, and one bead is placed on the first and last string.

Put the first bead on string 1 and make a Double Half Hitch. Then with each string from 2 to 14 make a Double Half Hitch on top of the wire. After string 14, put a bead on the wire.

You are now going to work the center pattern on strings 15, 16, 17, and 18, starting near the top of your work. Insert strings 16 and 17 together through a bead and then tie a Wing Knot one inch below the previous knot. Again leaving one inch, tie another Wing Knot below the first. Take string 15 and tie a Double Half Hitch over the wire. Next, place a bead on the wire and tie a Double Half Hitch with string 16. Do the same thing with strings 17 and 18, placing two more beads on the wire. After string 18, place another bead so that you will now have five beads on the wire in the center. Then, after you have completed the center, continue the Double Half Hitches until you reach the end, while following the shape of the wire. Remember to place a bead on the last string before tying the Double Half Hitch.

After all strings are knotted on the wire with Double Half Hitches, make another row of Double Half Hitches below the first row. These will, however, be knotted onto string and not onto wire, and both sides will be worked separately. Starting at the left-hand side, work the Double Half Hitches on top of the first string until the center is reached. Then working from the right-hand side toward the center, knot the Double Half Hitches onto the last string on the right (string 32).

You will then have two white strings which end at the center. Place one or two beads on the two white strings in the middle and tie a knot below the beads.

Cut the extra wire with pliers, one inch beyond the end of the Double Half Hitches, and turn both ends back behind the work. Then, cut the extra string as you wish.

Another Necklace

This second necklace is not built up on a wire foundation but has a knotted section to hang around the neck. White, red,

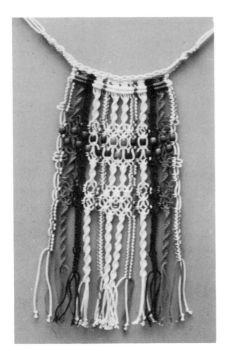

FIG. 88. *If no beads are available, this necklace can be made without them.*

and black string is used, together with green and red beads.

This project will work equally well with string in one color or several colors. Use wooden, cork, or ceramic beads in natural shades or in color. Remember that the ceramic beads break easily, and they are impossible to replace—unless you are willing to take the entire necklace apart.

Start with the neckband which consists of a length of spaced out Square Knots. Take four strings 4 yards long. Tie these together in the middle and make a length of knots working from the middle for 10 inches in both directions, so that you will have a band approximately 20 inches in length. The knots should be spaced out at intervals of about ¾ inch.

After you have completed the neckband, you are going to join both knotted ends together and add the colored strings to start the main body of the necklace. This time you are not working from a foundation string, but from the knots you already have. Put the two ends of the neckband together, facing you, and nail onto your worktable, leaving about 1½ inches between them. You now add the extra colored strings to these foundation knots. One double string should be added each time to form a diagonal shape. Two double, black strings 30 inches long should be added on the left side of the left-hand neck knot, and two double, red strings (also 30 inches long) on the right side. Pin or nail each time. Then add two, double, red strings to the left side of the right-hand neck knot and two, double, black strings to the right side. When adding these extra strings, the knots should all be tied close together.

The red strings are joined in the middle, when the third row of knots is tied, thus forming a V shape. Now pin your piece of work straight and continue knotting, leaving ¾ inch between all your knots, so that you have an effect of floating string. In the third row, insert a green bead on the middle strings for each knot you are making (five beads). In the fourth row, insert a red bead at each side and four green beads on the four center knots. In the fifth row, put one green bead in the middle and in the sixth row, put a green bead on each of the two center knots. The seventh row again has one green bead in the middle. The eighth row should have the knots closer to the preceding row (about ⅜ inch).

Now shape your work into an inverted V, working from the center toward the sides. Make two rows of Half Hitches. Take the two middle strings and put a green bead on them and then tie three Wing Knots and four regular knots with the four center strings below the bead.

Tie similar knots with the four white strings on each side of the center knots. Then, leaving two black strings loose on each

58

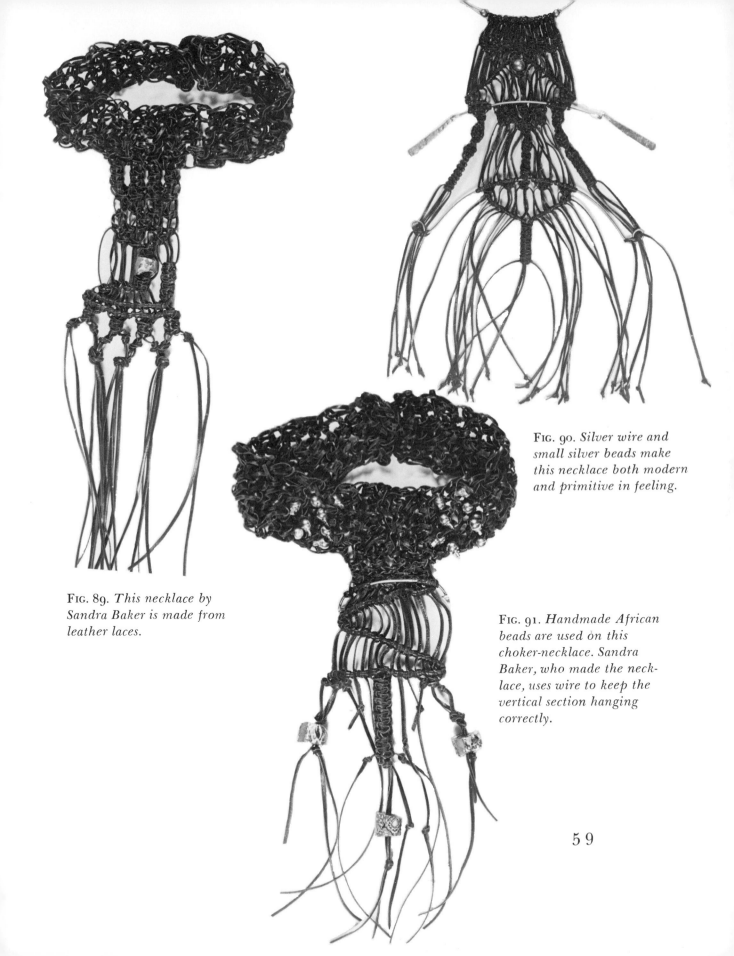

FIG. 90. *Silver wire and small silver beads make this necklace both modern and primitive in feeling.*

FIG. 89. *This necklace by Sandra Baker is made from leather laces.*

FIG. 91. *Handmade African beads are used on this choker-necklace. Sandra Baker, who made the necklace, uses wire to keep the vertical section hanging correctly.*

5 9

side, finish off the four outside strings. Put a red bead on each corner and tie three Wing Knots and six regular knots below it.

Leave the strings loose and cut the extra.

Headband

This headband is made with eight strings of nylon glow cord, 2 yards long. There are two red on each side and four yellow in the middle. Start knotting 15 inches from the end of your string. Make the first knot with the four yellow strings. Then, on each side, make a knot with the two red strings and two yellow. The next knot will be in the middle with the four yellow again. Repeat until you have six rows of knots, or approximately 5 inches; this brings you to the approximate center of your work. If you choose to substitute other colors in your own project, you may want to make a chart. The chart, with the correct color references, can be used as a guide.

The center section is tied in the following way, giving a raised effect. After tying the yellow knot, keep the two yellow fillers attached to the waist string or hook. Then, take the nearer red on each side and tie a red knot on top of the yellow. Next, take the two outside red strings and tie another knot, using the same fillers. The following knots are all tied on the same fillers:

Take the two side yellow strings and tie a knot.
Take the nearer red strings and tie a knot.
Knot the yellow strings.
Knot the next red strings.
Knot the yellow strings.
Knot the first red strings.
Knot the outside red strings.
Knot the yellow strings.

After this last yellow knot, make regular Square Knots as you did in the beginning. Repeat five or six times to match the other side. You can finish the ends with Double Half Hitches and cut the extra string according to your size.

Bracelet

The bracelet is made of cotton glow cord, size 0099, in blue, red, and yellow. Six double strings, or 12 ends 36 inches long,

FIG. 92. *Headbands, collars, chokers, bracelets, and watchbands are made in similar styles.*

FIG. 93. *Directions for the necklace can be found on pages 57–59. The bracelet can be worn on the upper or lower arm. The directions for the bracelet are on pages 60–61.*

are used, and the colors are arranged as follows: 2 yellow, 2 blue, 4 red, 2 blue, and 2 yellow. Of course, you may wish to use other colors.

You can start the bracelet like a belt, with each double string looped on another piece of cord, or on a buckle, if preferred. Make the first three rows of Square Knots and then shape your work to a point in the middle. You are now going to make the outside floating string design, combined with inside floating string, as in the belts described in chapter 4, figures 76–A and 76–B. Repeat your design five times, or until the bracelet fits your wrist. Finish it with one or two rows of Double Half Hitches. If you do not use a buckle, sew a button at one end and adjust according to size.

Headband or Choker

This design matches the bracelet for which instructions have been given. You can use the same number of strings and the same colors, but longer lengths. Take 6 double strings or 36 ends about 6 feet long. Begin 15 inches from the end of the string. Make the first two rows of knots and then shape your work to a point. Make the outside floating string design combined with inside floating string. Repeat three times; your work will then be in a pointed shape. Next, make two rows of Double Half Hitches on both sides of the point. The first row of Double Half Hitches takes the first string on the left (a yellow string) and drives it toward the center by making a Double Half Hitch on top of it with the other strings on the left—that is, strings 2, 3, 4, 5, and 6. Then, go to the right and take the last string and drive it to the center by making a Double Half Hitch on top of it with strings 11, 10, 9, 8, and 7.

Make a second row of Half Hitches by taking the first string on the left and the last string on the right and driving them toward the center. These knots are, of course, worked diagonally, and you will now have a double V shape. This design will be repeated as an inverted V shape, but before you do this, make two outside floating string patterns and one inside floating string pattern. Your work will then have the shape of an inverted V. Inside this shape, make two rows of Double Half Hitches, as before, but with the point facing in the other direction. Below the Double Half Hitches, make one row of Square Knots shaped like the inverted V. Repeat the inside and outside floating string design three times.

At both ends of your work, shape to a point. Make one or

FIG. 94. *A macramé headband and belt.*

61

FIG. 95. *This macramé skirt can be worn over a solid color underskirt, or for the more daring, over tights or a body stocking.*

two rows of Double Half Hitches, leaving the two center strings for tying at the back of the head, in the case of the headband, or behind the neck, in the case of the choker. Cut the other strings short and secure them with a needle and thread.

Skirts

Skirt 1. Take the waist measurement and loop double strings to fit the width of the waist, plus at least three inches. This skirt is a wrapped skirt, and the extra width allows for this. The first two rows must be knotted very tightly and close together to allow greater width at the level of the hips. It is recommended that the sides do not have an outside floating string design but be closely knotted to give greater strength and firmness. A simple diamond design, as shown in figure 95, makes a very effective skirt. Also, if an inside floating string design is used, the work will, of its own accord, tend to become wider as it progresses and will have the necessary lower width. The skirt is finished with a row of Double Half Hitches, following the line of the diamonds. At the points, make four Square Knots, one below the other. Cut the strings to the required length to form a fringe.

Skirt 2. The second skirt is made of cotton wrapping twine. It starts with Single Knots and then has five rows of inside floating string. Then, after loose knots for three inches, there fol-

FIG. 96.

FIG. 97. *A macramé outfit—headband, bracelet, and skirt.*

lows a row of sennits. In the center, the work is shaped to a point. Twenty inches of loose string are then left hanging free. This skirt is particularly effective worn over a simple black dress.

Macramé should be treated as any fine woven or knitted fabric. Try to avoid snags and pulls. However, if a bag or skirt does get snagged, you can ease the tension of the pulled fabric by laying the article on a firm backing and adjusting the pulled fiber.

You can wash macramé if it is made from nylon, wool, linen, cotton, or sisal twine. Any cold water detergent or soap will get the material clean. Soaking in mild soapsuds is probably the gentlest and best way to clean macramé. Soak the garment or object for about ten minutes in cool water. Brush any stubborn spots or heavy soil with an old toothbrush or a soft nail brush. Try not to rub too hard, as this will wear away the fibers of the twine. Rinse the macramé thoroughly in many rinse waters—preferably cool water. If you are washing a bag, belt, skirt, or other object that would be ruined if it were to shrink, block the macramé by pinning it to a towel in the shape that you want it to be.

Dry the macramé by hanging (if it is a wall hanging or belt), or by placing it flat on a rack or grid, so that the air can circulate freely about it. During the drying process, you may want to pull and shake the macramé into shape, to keep the knots sharp and free.

When you make a bag, be sure that the lining fabric is washable. And, if you knot a macramé belt on a buckle, be sure that the buckle is washable. Many people like wood buckles for just this reason. A wood buckle will never rust on the macramé of the belt.

Store most macramé flat. Exceptions might be large wall hangings and belts. However, heavy pieces of macramé will sag and change shape if they are stored on a hook or hung someplace. If the macramé is done in wool yarn, store it in a clean condition and in mothballs.

Sometimes you find old or worn pieces of macramé in "junk shops." If you do, and you would like to clean these pieces, follow the directions for washing.

Directions for dyeing macramé can be found on pages 77–81.

6

MACRAMÉ AS
AN ART FORM

AFTER having discussed some of the practical uses for macramé, we will turn to the most fascinating possibilities of this medium—macramé as an art form. Just as weaving can be done to make useful articles or can be developed into a serious art form, such as a medium for tapestries or wall hangings; so macramé can be utilitarian and practical or expressive and artistic.

Very large wall hangings similar to the hangings described in the second part of this chapter offer the craftsman tremendous possibilities in this area. These possibilities have, until now, been almost unexplored and scarcely developed. This lack of activity is probably due to the technical difficulties of handling the enormous amounts of cord and twine needed for the work, and the myriad string ends that seem tangled at the start of the work. The weight of the large hangings and the dimensions of the work are still other problems in "housekeeping" and work space. However, I have developed a way to overcome these problems, and I am offering my solutions for the first time in this book.

Of course, I am not suggesting that you start immediately on a very large wall hanging, or even with a room divider, but rather with a small wall hanging. The first wall hanging we will try measures 12 inches by 42 inches, and it is made of fisherman's Number 30 twine.

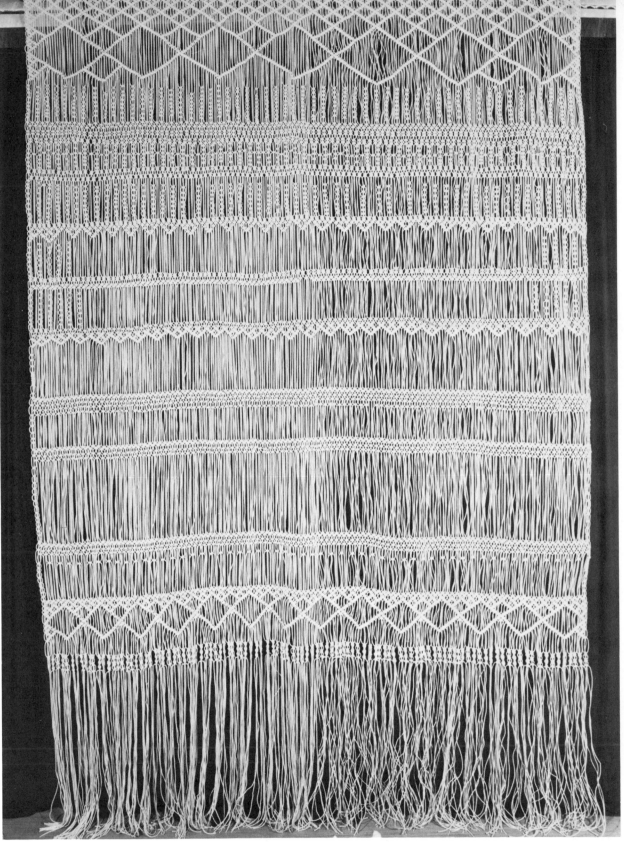

FIG. 98. *This wall hanging is made of white cotton twine and measures 6 feet by 10 feet. At the top there are small and large diamonds and below, bands of sennits combined with loose string. Lines of single and double knots divide the bands. At the bottom there is another diamond pattern, and the hanging is finished with spirals and loose fringe.*

This first venture into macramé as an art form should not give you a great deal of trouble, because the design is fairly simple—a combination of inside and outside floating string designs and Double Half Hitches. In addition, Instructions for another small wall hanging made of three different colors of string are also given.

First Macramé Wall Hanging

This wall hanging is made of 32 double strings, each of which will be 4 yards long. This will give you 64 ends, each 2 yards long, or 72 inches long. The hanging will be 16 knots wide.

Loop the double strings over a rod 16 inches long. The rod can be made of doweling or be part of a hanger. This rod can later be used to hang the finished piece of work.

While making a wall hanging, you will, of course, have large amounts of string lying on the floor. Unlike some macramé craftsmen, I definitely do *not* recommend that these strings be wound on bobbins. In fact, I advise against winding or gathering the string in any way. Leave the string on the floor. Even if the ends appear tangled, they will come free when you are ready to use them for tying a knot. It has been my experience that the strings easily come free, even when I have made very large wall hangings of six feet by ten feet. If you do have a problem, shake the string you wish to use. If it still does not easily untangle, hold the string in your hand and pick up the tangled mass of cord or twine and gently loosen the mass until your string comes loose and falls freely.

The following are step-by-step directions for the first wall hanging.

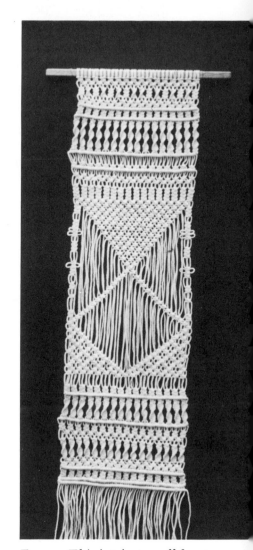

FIG. 99. *This intricate wall hanging measures 12 inches by 43 inches and is made of fine fisherman's twine. The design consists of bands of inside floating string diamonds, diagonal Half Hitches and sennits; then there are regular Square Knots set off by rows of horizontal Double Half Hitches.*

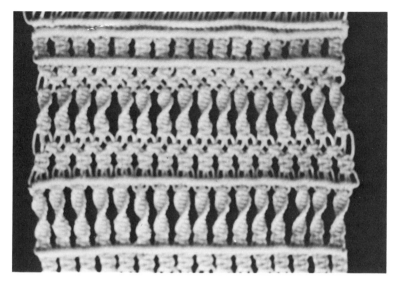

FIG. 100. *Detail, showing rows of sennits, of the top of the hanging featured in figure 99.*

Make 2 rows of Square Knots.

Row 3. Leave a ½-inch space below the knots on row 2. For the 1st, 3rd, 5th, 7th, 10th, 12th, 14th and 16th knots, make three Square Knots. The alternating knots, that is the 2nd, 4th, 6th, 8th, 9th (the two center knots), 11th, 13th, and 15th knots are six twisted Half Hitches.

Row 4. This row consists of Square Knots straight across your work, but ½ inch below Row 3.

Row 5. Regular Square Knots immediately below Row 4.

Row 6. Half Hitches across the work from left to right.

Row 7. A row of two Square Knots across the work.

Row 8. Half Hitches across the work from right to left.

Row 9. Twisted Half Hitches for approximately 2½ inches.

Row 10. Half Hitches across work from right to left.

Row 11. Leave a space of 1 inch and then work a row of Square Knots.

Row 12. Half Hitches across work from left to right.

Rows 13 and 14. Leave a space of ½ inch and then work 2 rows of single knots.

Row 15. Make a row of 4 knots, one below the other, across the work.

The Central Part of the Hanging

You now want to shape your work to a V, as for doing floating string. When you reach the last knot completing the V in the center of the work, you make two diagonal lines of single knots in both directions to the outside left and the outside right.

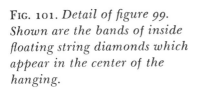

FIG. 101. *Detail of figure 99. Shown are the bands of inside floating string diamonds which appear in the center of the hanging.*

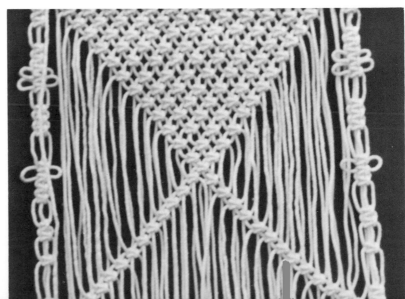

You will then have a kind of X shape. Leave 4 strings untied at each outside corner. Go back to the top corners of the floating string pattern and tie Wing Knots combined with single knots on these 4 strings, until you reach the bottom of your X shape. Join the strings to the diagonal lines with a single knot at each corner.

You are now going to complete an inside floating string diamond shape by two more diagonal rows of single knots meeting in the center. After that, fill up the sides with small diamonds until you have a horizontal line. Leave 1 inch.

The Lower Part of Hanging

Row 1. Make a row of 2 knots across your work.
Row 2. Double Half Hitches worked from right to left.
Row 3. A row of twisted Half Hitches for 2 inches.
Row 4. Double Half Hitches across work from right to left.
Row 5. Row of 2 knots across work ¼ inch below Row 4.
Row 6. Single row of knots across work.
Row 7. 1½ inches of twisted Half Hitches.
Row 8. Single row of knots.
Row 9. Single row of knots.
Row 10. Double Half Hitches worked from left to right.
Row 11. A row of 2 knots.
Rows 12 and 13. Two rows of Double Half Hitches.
Cut extra string evenly at desired length.

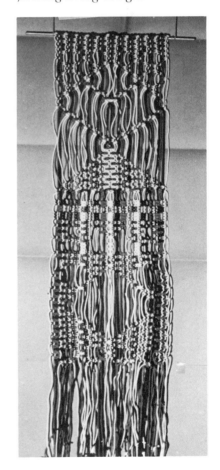

FIG. 102. *A wall hanging utilizing red, white, and black twine and incorporating an inside floating string design.*

Multicolored Wall Hanging

This wall hanging can be made with string of three colors—white, black, and red—or you can choose any other three colors. If you do choose three other colors, you may wish to make a chart so that the color substitution will be easier to follow.

To begin your multicolored wall hanging, take 34 double strings 5 feet long, 12 white, 11 black, and 11 red. Loop them on top of another separate piece of string or a quarter-inch rod. Place them in this order: white, black, and red. Repeat until you have all the strings set, and so that it will end with a double white string.

Make three rows of knots and shape your work to an inverted V. Then make the first row of inside floating string design so that you have a total of 8 small diamond shapes. On your second row you are going to make only 3 small diamond shapes—that is, the second, the fourth, and the sixth. You leave a space where you would expect to make the first, third, fifth, and seventh inside floating string design.

You will now find that by doing this you will have wider inverted V shapes with 5 knots on each side. Here you now make four larger diamond shapes. While doing this, you must be particularly careful to keep your work even.

Before making the fourth row, divide your work into two parts at the center and work each side separately from the center to the left-hand side and from the center to the right-hand side. Make the inside and outside floating string design until you reach the last knot at each corner. You will now have a very wide inverted V. Make a row of Double Half Hitches along the inverted V.

Then, starting from the corner, count 8 knots each side of the inverted V. Make a larger diamond by making a row of knots, working diagonally toward the center. Below this, make a row of Double Half Hitches.

Go back to the left-hand corner and make a row of knots going diagonally to the center. Then repeat from the right-hand side and join at the center. You will now have a large diamond stretching right across the hanging with a smaller diamond inside it. After this row, make a row of Double Half Hitches.

Below the large diamond, you are going to have a design of closely worked knots in the center and loose, floating string on the outside. Make one Square Knot in the center of your work and divide it into two parts. Make the outside floating string design by working a row of knots, going diagonally from the center to the left, and from the center to the right. You will then have a large inverted V stretching right across your work. Fill up the middle of the inverted V with the small diamond design, as in the first row of inside floating string design at the top of the work. When the V has been completely filled and you have a straight row of 8 small inverted V's, make a zigzag row of Double Half Hitches across the work. Move your work one inch back and secure it on the working area. Make a row of two knots and then make a row of three knots. Repeat this design five times and then divide your work into two parts again. Shape to a big inverted V by making a row of knots diagonally from the center to the left-hand side and then from the center to the right-hand side. You may wish to build up the sides with inside floating string design, as at the top, or vary it in some other way.

Finish your big diamond by making a row of knots diagonally from the left-hand side to the center and from the right-hand side to the center. Join and fill up both sides of the pointed shape with small diamonds. At the bottom, shape your work so that you have four medium-size diamonds. Then, make two rows of single knots.

Finish your hanging with a row of Double Half Hitches and cut the extra cord.

LARGE WALL HANGINGS AND ROOM DIVIDERS

If you have been able to make a belt, a handbag, and a small wall hanging, then you can also make a large, one-piece wall hanging or room divider. It is not easy, but it is not especially difficult either. Some craftsmen produce a large piece of work by making it in sections, which they later join together. This is similar to the way in which many Africans do their weaving on very narrow looms. Afterward, five or six pieces are sewn

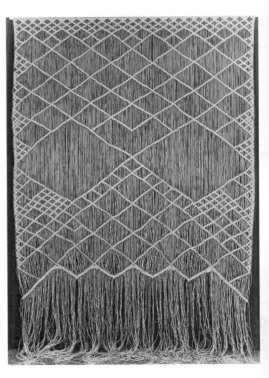

FIG. 103. *This wall hanging or room divider is made of linen twine and measures 6 feet by 10 feet. The design consists of diamonds of varying sizes, including two measuring 20 inches by 20 inches. The hanging is finished with Double Half Hitches following the line of diamonds. At the bottom there is a 2-foot fringe. This hanging is particularly effective when used as a room divider, where it can hang in an open space.*

FIG. 104. *Close-up of a large 20-inch by 20-inch diamond which constitutes half of the main focal point in the design of the hanging in figure 103.*

together lengthwise to make a beautiful rug. Some very fine wall hangings can be made by joining sections of macramé together, but if you have the ability and the knowledge to do your work in one piece, the result is far more satisfying, as well as being stronger. More important is the fact that such a work has an artistic unity which a work sewn together in strips can never possess.

Width

By now, you will have noticed that a Square Knot varies in size according to the thickness of the string you use. It can measure as little as $\frac{1}{8}$ inch or as much as one inch or more. In other words, the number of knots you will need to make a wall hanging of a certain size will depend upon the thickness of the string. If you have planned a definite size and know which string you are going to use, take four pieces of that string, make a Square Knot and measure it. If it measures one inch, you should multiply 4 by 60, so that for a wall hanging 60 inches wide, you will need 240 strings or 120 double strings. It can sometimes happen that you may need more or fewer knots to reach your width of 60 inches, according to whether you tie your knots tightly or loosely. I should advise you to loop all your double strings on a rod, wire, or string and make the first row of knots until you have reached the width you want.

FIG. 105. *This is a small but elaborate wall hanging. The size is 12 inches by 20 inches, and the material is white cotton twine. The design consists of diagonal and horizontal Double Half Hitches combined with single knots.*

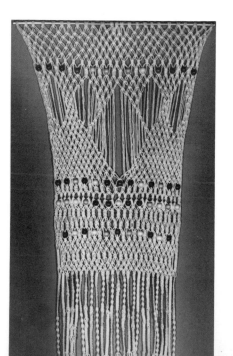

FIG. 106. *This wall hanging, which measures 24 inches by 42 inches, is mounted on a rod and consists mainly of loose knots. Following a row of multi-colored wooden beads, there is an inside floating string design. A large central diamond has two smaller diamonds on each side; then follow two more rows of beads. After two rows of double knots, there is a last row of beads and another band of loose knots. The hanging is finished with lines of sennits and spirals forming a knotted fringe.*

It is not only the width but also the length which must be considered before the wall hanging can be started. I must stress that it is far better to have longer strings than you need, rather than the contrary. It is tedious to have to add string, unless it is absolutely necessary. Also, you must know the right moment to do it. For example, two strings must never be added at the same knot, because this would make the work very bulky. I personally use four times the length I plan for my finished work. This is not because I am afraid to add string, but rather because it requires considerable concentration to do it correctly, and adding string is therefore time consuming.

In chapter 7, I discuss the warping reel used by weavers and also the warping frame. Not many macramé craftsmen use these, as the majority are not weavers. The warping reel is, however, by far the most convenient tool for an advanced craftsman who does large-scale macramé. If you do not have a warping reel, it is not an insurmountable handicap; it will, however, take you considerably longer to measure each double string by hand.

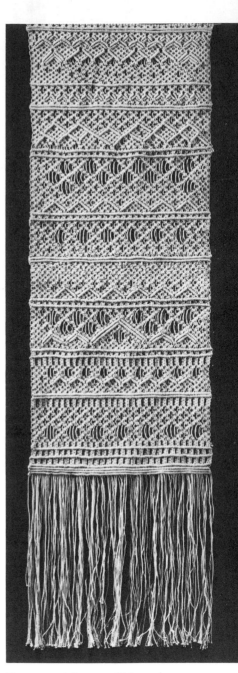

FIG. 107. *A long wall hanging featuring diagonal and horizontal Double Half Hitches, combined with single knots and rows of inside floating string diamonds. The work is finished with a long string of fringe.*

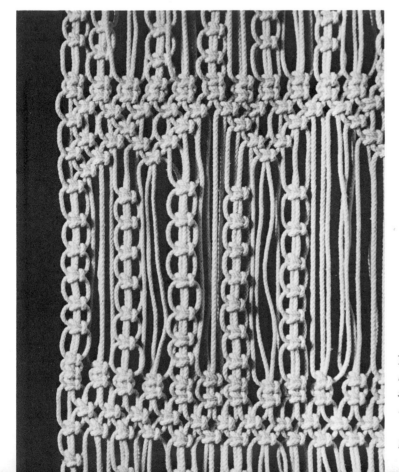

FIG. 108. *Detail of a large wall hanging (see fig. 98) showing single knots (also called loose knots or space knots) at half-inch intervals, combined with floating string.*

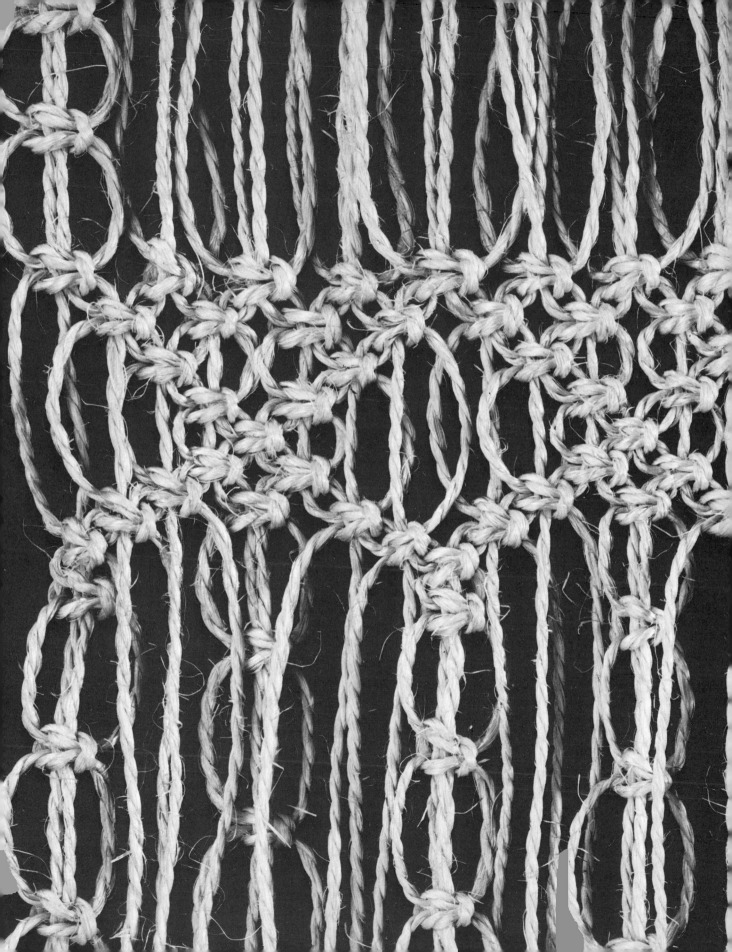

To start with, you must have a clear idea in your mind of the width and length of the piece you are going to make. Your working area will depend upon the dimensions of your finished hanging. Your working base must extend at least one inch beyond your work on both sides. In this way you can control the edges. For instance, if you are making a piece 60 inches wide, it is better to have a working foundation measuring 62 inches or more. It is possible to use string for this, but it is more satisfactory if the work is looped over a rod. This rod can later be used to hang the finished work.

It is not always easy to choose a suitable working area, as it is vitally important that a large-scale piece of macramé should be left completely undisturbed until it is finished. As it may take several months to complete, this can lead to problems. However, the craftsman should take such factors into account before embarking on such a piece of work. If it is possible to monopolize one room for this purpose, the results make any trouble caused very worthwhile.

The strings should be left on the floor, just as they are. They may be stepped on, if necessary, but should not be lifted or moved, because if disturbed, they get tangled. I most strongly recommend that the student should not use bobbins: the labor involved in winding bobbins is enormous, and this time can more profitably be used in knotting.

After the space problem has been solved, the next question is the table or other base on which to work. If a table of suitable size can be spared, this can be used. If not, a couch can very satisfactorily be used as a base. This has a great advantage in that the work can be pinned to the back of the couch and easily moved backward. Regular pins may be used, but T pins are better. You can sit behind the couch, and the finished work can rest on the seat of the couch. For a very long hanging, after a certain length has been reached, the most satisfactory results are obtained if the piece of work can hang from the ceiling. Three or four hooks placed in the ceiling will allow the work on its rod to hang down with the slack on the seat of a couch or on the back of a table. This makes it easier to control the work. You can also judge your design better and make any necessary modifications.

75

FIG. 109. *Detail of an 8-foot by 12-foot sisal wall hanging.*

Loop your double strings on a rod about 65 inches to 70 inches long and make the first row of Square Knots. Measure the width to see if you have the right number of strings for the hanging you are planning. Then make the second and third rows of Square Knots so that you have a solid foundation on which to start your design. After that, you can plan what kind of design you wish to make. I do not recommend a very complicated design for a large hanging, as it could take many months to complete. If you plan a hanging consisting mainly of inside and outside floating string, after the third row, you can start building a row of inverted shapes. After this, you can make small diamonds and then larger ones. You can even have diamonds measuring as much as 20 inches by 20 inches as on the linen room divider shown in figure 102. You can also leave large areas on string unknotted, as on the cotton twine room divider. However, great care must be taken to keep your work even. You must be certain to move your work back an exactly equal distance all the way across, otherwise your work will be lopsided. You will find that your work is extremely flexible, and in order to control it, it must be pinned at frequent intervals. If you do not pin it very firmly, you may find that your knots are crooked and that your work does not follow the shape you have planned.

When making a very large floating string diamond (20 inches by 20 inches) it is advisable to have a small stool or bench, with a cushion on top, to hold the loose string from the diamond. If you have a bench of the same width as the couch, it is particularly helpful in controlling the shape of the design.

It can sometimes happen that despite all one's care, the work is uneven or a mistake is made. It is then advisable to move the work and leave an area of loose string from 5 inches to 10 inches wide. Pin your work above this free area but be particularly careful to do this in a straight line. Then, make a horizontal row of Square Knots across your work before starting a new section of your design.

FINISHING THE WALL HANGING

If your wall hanging is made up of diamond shapes, make a row of Double Half Hitches following the diamonds. The remaining string should be evenly cut, but it makes a good finish to a wall hanging to leave a fringe of about one foot.

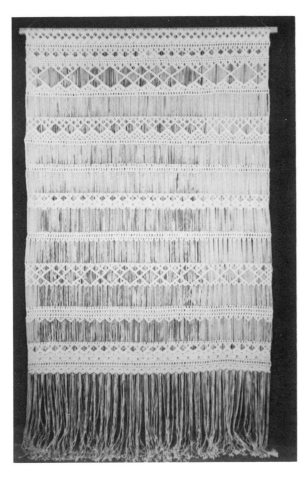

FIG. 110. *This superb macramé wall hanging measures 8 feet by 10 feet. At the top there is a design of small and medium diamonds. A band of loose strings has a line of small diamonds below it. Variations of this diamond theme are repeated, and the hanging is finished by a long string fringe.*

If your design is not built up mainly on diamond shapes, finish your hanging with a straight line of Double Half Hitches. Leave a fringe as before.

Dyes and Dyeing Your Own Materials

String, twine, and yarn are usually dyed in large quantities in factories, and most craftsmen buy their material ready-dyed. It is, of course, easier to buy ready-dyed twine and time-saving to select the exact shade you need from the display in a store. However, it is a very good experience and often extremely rewarding (if you have the time and space available) to dye your own materials. You can experiment with color and with different tones or shades; you can try new shades and different combinations of colors, and it can be lots of fun.

There are two types of dyeing that may be done at home. The simpler method is to buy one of the powdered or liquid dyes that are obtainable in a large selection of colors. You can usually find these dyes at grocery stores, drug stores, and five-and-ten-cent stores. Rit dye is one of the easiest to use, and directions are included on every bottle or package.

Many hand weavers and macramé knotters prefer to use natural vegetable dyes or compound their own dyes. Vegetable dyes impart beautiful soft colors that are not possible with chemical dyes.

Until the middle of the nineteenth century, vegetable dyes were universally used, but with the discovery of commercially produced aniline dyes, their use died out almost completely. Recently, there has been a resurgence of interest in using plant material for dyeing. Considerable work has been done in this field in the Brooklyn Botanical Gardens, where plant dyeing is taught. They have published an excellent handbook, *Dye Plants and Dyeing*, which shows how many wild and garden plants can be used to produce colors suitable for use in either weaving or macramé. Some of these plants, such as ladies' bedstraw for red; broom, privet, or marigold for yellow; bracken for green, and walnut for dark brown, are readily available. Others, including indigo for blue, madder for red, and logwood for blue-gray or black, should be obtained in one of the stores specializing in dyes and herbs. Some of these commercial suppliers are listed on pages 136 and 137. Before the actual dyeing, the skeins of yarn or string should be mordanted. A mordant is a preparation that combines with the dye substance to form an insoluble compound and to fix the color in the textile. Without a mordant, the dye would come out of the fabric as soon as it was washed or became wet for any reason. The process of mordanting allows the dye to take properly and to retain its color.

Substances such as alum, iron vitriol, and chrome are often used as mordants for textiles. After mordanting, the skeins of textile materials—yarn, twine, cord, or fabric—are immersed in the actual dye bath and then allowed to soak, simmer, boil, or rot, according to the recipe. Afterward, the twine or yarn is rinsed and dried, and the dyed and colorful material is ready for use.

The following directions and recipes for natural vegetable dyes first appeared in *Foot-Power Loom Weaving* by Edward Worst in 1919, but the directions and formulas are equally good today.[1]

1. Edward Worst, *Foot-Power Loom Weaving* (Milwaukee: The Bruce Publishing Company, 1919), pp. 202–216.

Yellow

Yarn   250 g. (8 oz.)
Alum* (mordant)   32 g. (4 heaping tablespoons or 1 oz.)
Fresh bayberry leaves   500 g. (1 lb. and 1 oz.)
   Mordant before dyeing. Boil the leaves one hour, drain, add material, and boil one hour.

Dark Red

Yarn   250 g. (8 oz.)
Cream of tartar (mordant)   16 g. (2 tablespoons)
Alum (mordant)   65 g. (8 tablespoons)
Madder   250 g. (10 tablespoons) (8 oz.)
   Mordant the yarn for two hours and let it remain in the liquid until cool. Rinse in lukewarm water. The twine or yarn may be allowed to dry after removing it from the mordant; then it is rinsed in warm water before it is put into the madder liquid. The day before it is to be used, the madder should be put to soak in enough cold water to make a very thin solution. If there are hard lumps, they must be rubbed apart in order to soak thoroughly. When ready to dye, put the soaked madder mass in clean cold water, and when lukewarm, add the mordanted yarn. Heat slowly to 60 or 70 degrees centigrade, or hot enough to burn one's fingers. Stir the yarn constantly and keep the solution at the same temperature as long as the yarn is in it. *It must not boil.* If the yarn is not stirred, it becomes spotted, as the part of madder liquid that heats the most quickly gives the strongest color. The red coloring matter in the madder dissolves without boiling, but with boiling, the other ingredients in the madder are also dissolved and these may cause the red color to lose its brightness and to change to brown. When the yarn has been in the madder liquid for about twenty minutes, turn off the stove, or take the pot to a place for cooling. Keep stirring until the material is cool. Wash the material in several waters to remove the loose madder. All dark madder colors remain fast. However, the lighter colors may fade a little as the years go by.

   * Alum is a useful mordant for most vegetable dyes. When alum is used, it must be boiled in order to become thoroughly dissolved. All goods must be wet before entering the mordant. When mordanting, all the material should be well covered with the mordant liquid.

Red

Yarn   250 g. (8 oz.)
Alum (mordant)   40 g. (5 tablespoons)
Cream of tartar (mordant)   16 g. (2 tablespoons)
Bed straw roots   250 g. (8 oz.)

Mordant the yarn from 1 to 2 hours. The dry roots are ground or chopped fine and put to soak for a few hours. The dyeing of the yarn is the same as was described for dark red, using the madder coloring, except that the yarn is boiled a little toward the end of the dyeing process.

Dark Blue with Chickweed

Yarn   250 g.
Fresh chickweed   1 pail
Alum (mordant)   32 g. (4 tablespoons)
Logwood   50 g. (3½ tablespoons)

The logwood should be put to soak the day before it is to be used. Place it in a bag and boil it in clear water for one hour and then remove from the water. Boil the chickweed in water for one hour and drain. Add the alum to the liquid used for boiling the chickweed and stir well. Take the wet, unmordanted yarn and add to the liquid. Boil the yarn for one hour and then take it from the liquid. During the boiling of the yarn, add a small bag filled with the soaked logwood and leave it in the boiling liquid for one-half hour. Add the yarn and let it boil one hour with the logwood bag. Allow the yarn to remain in the liquid until it is cool. If a darker dye is wanted, use more logwood.

Dyeing of Predyed or Your Own Materials

If you wish to dye old, faded, or predyed goods, they must first be well washed and then boiled for one-half hour in soda water. This will remove as much of the original dye as possible. When old goods are dyed, a darker color than the original must be chosen. For success, a great deal depends on the foundation color, as the new color must be dark enough to cover the old.

Only pale yellow or pink may be dyed yellow. Pale yellow, pale violet, light gray, light brown, and light green may be dyed red. Pale yellow, pale green, violet, blue gray, and light brown may be dyed blue.

Mixtures of yellow and blue dyes can be used to obtain green. Mixtures of red and yellow dyes may be used to impart an orange or bronze color. Reds and blues can be used to obtain violets and purples.

Most light colors may be dyed brown, which can be made from green, red, and yellow. All colors, light or dark, may be dyed black. It must be understood that with redyeing, the new color, unless very light, will always have a tone of the original or ground color.

PART TWO

Weaving

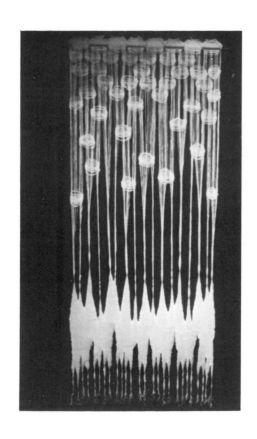

7

WOVEN WALL
HANGINGS

Introduction

WEAVING is one of the most ancient crafts known to mankind; in fact, the production of woven clothing was one of man's first steps on the path to civilization. The craft of weaving has changed remarkably little, and the primitive looms found all over the world are basically very similar to looms used by craftsmen today. In this respect, the textile departments of museums are very interesting, and the weavings to be found there are a fruitful source of inspiration to weavers of today.

As all weavers know, weaving is a supremely satisfying occupation. You do not need to be a great weaver to make tapestries or wall hangings, and they offer an opportunity to do really creative work. You do, however, need to know the basic elements of weaving, and a few simple techniques which you can learn by yourself, just in the way that our ancestors did thousands of years ago—first, through necessity, and second, through making slow progress day by day and year by year.

The earliest looms were probably nothing more than two small branches—one tied to the bottom of a tree and the other to the weaver's waist. The warp would have been made with either long palm leaves or the bark of other trees, and the weft with smaller leaves or grass. From this must have developed the

FIG. 111. *Exciting and beautiful tapestry can be woven on a small loom.*

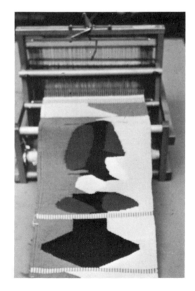

first form of frame loom. Later, there came hand looms and then foot looms, until finally the power loom was invented with its many elaborate variations such as the jacquard loom.

Even a five-year-old child can learn to weave on an inkle loom or a frame loom. A frame loom, which in many ways is ideally suited for tapestry weaving, is nothing more than a simple wooden shape like a picture frame. It consists of four pieces of wood nailed together to form a rectangle. Canvas stretchers, which can be bought in any art supply store, are very suitable; a good size for a beginner would be 16 inches by 20 inches or 20 inches by 30 inches. However, for an adult interested in weaving, I would suggest buying a table loom or a floor loom.

The craft of weaving can be developed in various directions: the loom can be set up to make a number of elaborate patterns such as the Rosepath, Monk's Belt, or Honeysuckle. These patterns are admirably suited for making table runners, mats, cushion covers, bags, and similar articles. However we are interested in weaving as an art form rather than as a suitable medium

FIG. 112. *A table loom.*

FIG. 113. *A floor loom in Yvonne Forbach's studio.*

FIG. 114. *A corner of Yvonne Forbach's studio, showing some experimental work.*

for useful articles. For our purpose, we suggest that a knowledge of straight draw, or plain draw (as it is often called), tapestry weave, and double weave will lead to the production of beautiful wall hangings. These are not elaborate techniques, and once you have a basic knowledge of weaving, these simple techniques can be quickly mastered. In weaving, color, texture, and overall design are of primary importance, rather than intricate detail.

PREPARATIONS FOR WEAVING

The Warp

Before you prepare your warp, you must calculate exactly how much you need. To do this, you multiply the width of the hanging you intend to make by the number of threads per inch. For example, if your hanging is to be twenty inches wide, and you are going to weave 12 threads per inch, you will need 240 ends. To this you add two extra threads on each side to

FIG. 115. *A warping reel with multiple spool rack.*

make a firm selvage, so that altogether you will have 240 + 4, that is, 244 ends.

After calculating the number of ends, you must calculate the length. There is always considerable wastage when weaving, and this must be allowed for. To save work, and also not to waste more warp than necessary, it is quite a good idea to weave more than one hanging on the same warp. You must then remember to allow some extra warp for the space between your two pieces of work. You should allow approximately one yard extra warp for tying to the rollers on the front and back beams of the loom. In other words, if you make a three-yard warp you will be able to make two wall hangings, each 30 inches long, with some extra warp for fringes between the two hangings.

There are various methods of measuring the yarn for the warp. For small pieces with shorter warps, a warping frame can be used. This is rather like a picture frame with pegs along the sides. The yarn is wound around the pegs until the desired length is reached. If no equipment is available, it is possible to use two high-backed chairs, if weights are placed on the chairs so that they do not move.

By far the most satisfactory method, especially for longer warps, is the warping reel. As mentioned in chapter 6, this can also be used for measuring string for macramé. The reel rotates as the yarn is wound, so that the necessary length of warp can be wound quite quickly. One rotation from top to bottom produces a three-yard length; two rotations a six-yard length. While you are winding the warp, it is best to have your yarns on spools on a spool rack. Figure 115 shows both a warping reel and a spool rack.

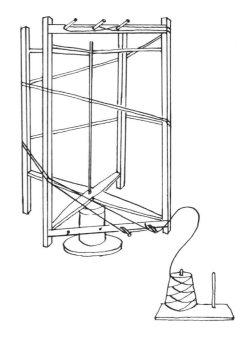

FIG. 116. *Warping reel and spool rack.*

Setting up the Loom

We are assuming that the reader has some knowledge of the basic elements of weaving, but since it is sometimes difficult to remember the different steps in setting up the loom correctly, they will be described very briefly.

It will be noticed that at the top and bottom of the warping reel a cross has been formed by the yarn being wound around the pegs. Before removing the warp from the reel, this cross must be secured by tying firmly with thread of a different color. After this has been done, the warp may be removed by knotting it loosely in a chain, just like a crocheted chain, but using the hand instead of a crochet hook.

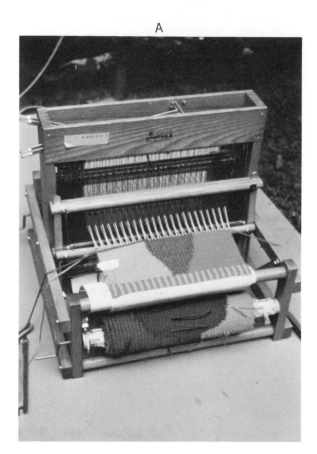
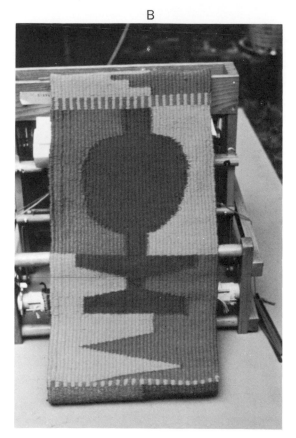

FIG. 117. *Woven tapestry. A: On loom; B: Off the loom.*

The next step is to transfer the warp chain to the loom. Some people thread the loom from the back, while others prefer to do it from the front. I shall describe how to do it from the front, but you can, of course, do it from the back, if that is what you are accustomed to doing.

Tie double strings on each side of the loom from the back beam to the front beam to hold the warp sticks. Put the warp sticks through each side of the cross of the warp with the short end of the warp facing the front. Tie the sticks together on each side.

Wrap the long end of the warp around the back beam and tie very firmly with a piece of string. Cut the end of the warp so that you have a number of ends to thread.

Count the heddles from the middle to the side according to the number of ends in your warp, leaving the extra heddles on each side. Thread the heddles using a threading hook. For

FIG. 118.
Working with a table loom.

FIG. 119.
Working with a floor loom.

tapestry, double weave, and many other types of wall hangings, straight draw will be used. That is, you thread the heddles: 1 – 2 – 3 – 4 in order. Tie the ends as you go, in groups of twenty or so. After threading the heddles, place the reed (without the beater) flat across the loom, between the two strings on the side of the loom. Thread the yarn down through the reed dents. Replace the reed dents in the beater.

The next step is to tie the warp threads to the rod on the cloth roller attached to the front beam. These threads are tied very evenly in small groups.

The warp must then be untied from the back beam and wound to the front beam. This must be done very slowly and evenly. As you go, shake hard to disentangle the warp. This must never be forced. If it does not go smoothly, examine the warp to see if there is a knot, or if the heddles are twisted and causing the obstruction. Stop before you have finished winding the warp to the front (about 1½ to 2 feet before the end); disentangle the ends and tie them to the back beam. Use Half Knots first and then bows. Remove the warp sticks and strings from the sides.

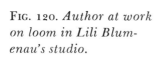

FIG. 120. *Author at work on loom in Lili Blumenau's studio.*

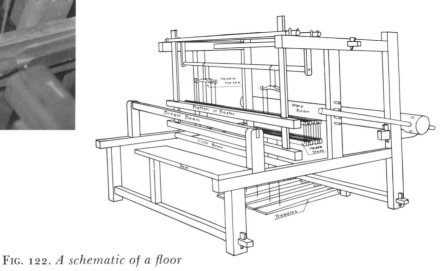

FIG. 121. *A tapestry in the making on a floor loom.*

FIG. 122. *A schematic of a floor loom.*

Reverse the warp by winding it onto the back beam, using sheets of brown wrapping paper as you go to keep the warp even. Loosen the warp in the front and retie to the front beam. This will control the tension of your warp. When you have finished this operation, you should check the loom to see that there are no mistakes. Do this by raising shafts 1 and 3 and then shafts 2 and 4, and inserting sticks. Check with a yarn of contrasting color. If all is correct, you are then ready to start weaving.

93

We have suggested straight draw as being suitable for wall hangings. However, a plain piece of weaving with straight draw would not make a very interesting wall hanging. Once the weaver begins to vary the colors and textures in his weft, he will produce more interesting hangings. Yarns of different thicknesses can be used to add interest. It is probably the imaginative use of colors which is of the greatest importance in making wall hangings.

The weaver can experiment with a variety of yarns in making wall hangings. Hand-spun Haitian cotton, for example, produces a very attractive texture when woven and blends well with other yarns. Yarns of different weights can be used, and also novelty yarns such as loop yarns or nub yarns.

Many weavers do not restrict their materials to yarns, but use natural materials such as grasses, reeds, seeds, feathers, and canes. Joyce Griffiths has used heads of wheat and barley in combination with leno techniques in a very effective hanging (fig. 124). Pieces of ceramic by Michael Hardy have been used in Mike Halsey's fine wall hanging (fig. 125). The weaver should make his own experiments with a variety of materials.

FIG. 123. Cross and Sun. *Wall hanging. Lili Blumenau.*

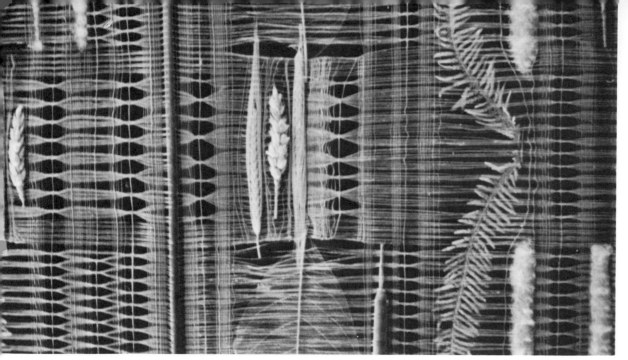

FIG. 124. Leno weaving. *The warp is linen and fine mercerized cotton; weft is linen, mercerized cotton, wheat and barley heads with white fleece and leaves. Joyce Griffiths.*

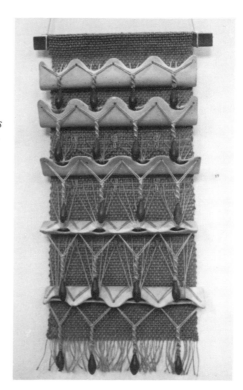

FIG. 125. Ceramic and Textile Hanging. *This hanging is 12 inches by 24 inches. It includes ceramic pieces made by Michael Hardy and lead fishing weights. Mike Halsey.*

Open spaces can be an interesting part of wall hangings. For example, an area can be left unwoven and the warp threads left floating or tied in some way. This can be seen in the hanging illustrated in figure 126. Other weavers use open spaces in the form of slits separating narrow bands of weaving. These narrow bands must, of course, be woven with a short shuttle.

The beginner normally starts with plain weave and learns to beat it down regularly to form a solid tight texture. Plain weave can, however, be approached in a completely different way. The hanging *Sea and Land* is an example of this.

Wall Hanging—Sea and Land

This hanging, which measures 15 inches by 32 inches, has a warp of white cotton twine. A 12-dent reed is used, and there are 360 ends. The loom is threaded in straight draw, and plain weave is used throughout. The two-color weft is of white and dark brown cotton. Weave about 1 inch in white cotton and then insert a bamboo rod. Then weave 4 inches of solid texture, using the beater.

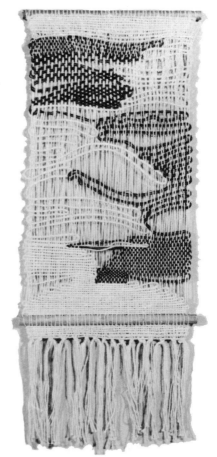

FIG. 126. Sea and Land. *A wall hanging 15 inches by 32 inches.*

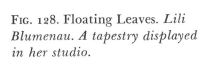

Fig. 127. *Wall hanging by the author. Seven feet by 45 inches.*

Fig. 128. Floating Leaves. *Lili Blumenau. A tapestry displayed in her studio.*

Next, start shaping your weft and no longer use the beater but a fork instead. One side of your work should be brown and the other white. With the fork, the weft can be shaped into a curve resembling a hill. After about 8 inches, the white cotton is woven right across to make the piece firmer. The white cotton then remains on the left, while the brown is taken over to the right to produce a balanced composition of color. Continue weaving loosely, according to your design. Loose, unwoven warp is, for the most part, left in the middle. Smaller areas of loose warp may be left at the sides, but care should be taken not to spoil the tension. In any case, the areas of loose warp should be balanced so that all the loose warp is not on one side.

At the end, weave firmly straight across, using the beater. Insert another rod and then weave another 3 inches. When the hanging is removed from the loom, do not cut the warp from the front beam. This will allow you to make long fringes or a macramé edging, as described in the next chapter.

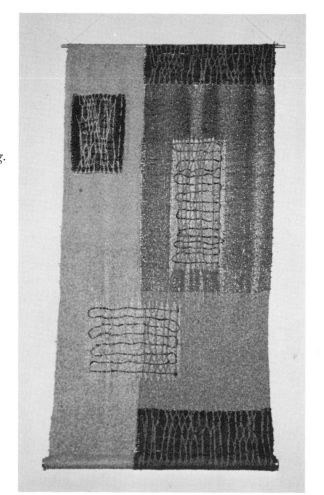

FIG. 129. *A colorful and imaginative wall hanging.*

9 8

Experimental Wall Hangings

In recent years there has been a considerable amount of experimental work in weaving, and there have been a number of developments in the direction of three-dimensional work which bear a certain affinity to sculpture. One of the foremost British weavers, Peter Collingwood, has done a series of hangings entitled *Macrogauze*, one of which is shown here (fig. 131). Some weavers start their experimental work with double cloth, which is then opened out with canes or rods inserted at various angles to give it shape. Many pieces of work can no longer be called wall hangings, as they stand free and are no longer bound to the wall. Normal weaving techniques are not used, but sometimes knotting and weaving techniques on free-hanging warps. Experimental textiles of this kind can sometimes be seen in exhibitions, and these can give both advanced and beginning weavers ideas for imaginative work.

FIG. 131. Microgauze 63. *Made in black linen with stainless steel rod. Peter Collingwood.*

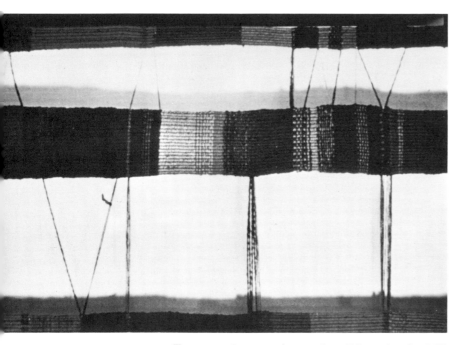

FIG. 130. *An experimental wall hanging by Lili Blumenau.*

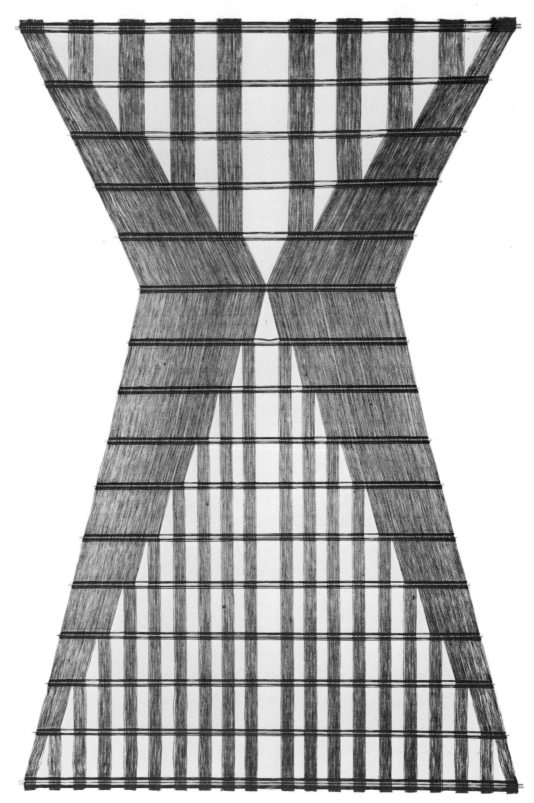

Macrogauze 33. *Peter Collingwood.*

WEAVING AND MACRAMÉ

THERE are some exciting opportunities for the artist-craftsman in combining weaving with macramé. In any case, the weaver is advised to acquire some knowledge of macramé, as macramé forms an admirable finish to a woven wall hanging, as well as other pieces of hand weaving. There is always a considerable length of warp which cannot be woven, as it is used for tying to the front or back beam. When the piece of weaving is removed from the loom, do not cut this extra warp and throw it away (which many weavers do). The warp can be used to make a beautiful part of the hanging—a macramé fringe.

For the craftsman who is primarily interested in macramé, a knowledge of the basic elements of weaving can allow him great scope and variety in making many macramé articles, including wall hangings. For the craftsman working in this medium, the woven section would probably be quite short—possibly only a small part or one third of the total piece—and the chief emphasis in design and texture would be on the macramé section.

When making a hanging in which macramé predominates, it is always wise to choose a weaving design which harmonizes with macramé. I prefer to use straight draw, combination draw,

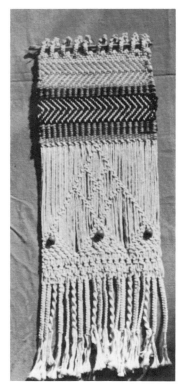

FIG. 132. *A colorful wall hanging of intricate woven design, set off by a stunning macramé fringe.*

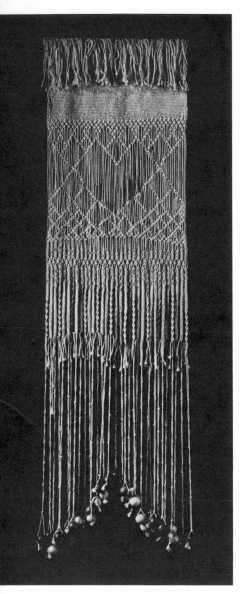

FIG. 133. *A hanging with macramé predominating and har-
monizing with the woven part.*

or point draw. I would suggest your woven part could be about one third of the piece of work you are making, and the macramé about two thirds. Thus, on a three-yard warp, I would weave about one foot for the upper woven area, and then take it off the loom. If there are many Double Half Hitch knots in your macramé design, you will need at least this amount of string for working. For such a project, I would not advise you to use fine thread for the warp. It would be better to use 16-ply cotton or 3-ply linen, unless you are sure that you have enough experience and patience to handle the finer warp thread.

Even if you are going to weave only 10 inches of your three-yard warp, you must still set the loom in the normal way. And there is another important point you must remember. You must also make sure that the number of warp threads you have is divisible by four. If you do this, you will not have to add any extra ends for the macramé after you have taken your work off the loom.

After finishing the woven part—10 inches, 20 inches, or whatever length you make it—you must take the weaving off the loom to do the macramé. To do this, untie the front beam and then unroll the back beam. Untie the back ends, and then pull off four threads at a time from the reed and heddles until you have reached the end. In this way you will avoid the warp becoming tangled. Next, place the woven area on a straight line, on a table or other suitable working place. Divide your string into groups of four, and after nailing the weaving to a piece of backing wood, start your macramé.

First Woven Wall Hanging with Macramé

This is quite a small wall hanging done in tapestry technique. As in the macramé in chapters 5 and 6, you can use the colors that you like best. I've suggested certain colors and they work well, but don't hesitate to substitute your own. The wide macramé fringe changes it from a rather ordinary piece of weaving into a decorative hanging. Natural colored 2-ply linen is used for the warp. The hanging is 20 inches wide, and there are 144 ends. An 8-dent reed is used. The weft is made of heavy 3-ply tapestry yarn in dark purple, gray, and blue-green. Leno technique is used in the center area, which measures 10 inches by 16 inches. In this technique, the loose warp threads are tied in groups by passing left over right and right over left. Every

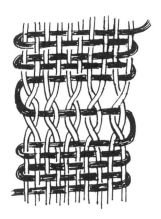

FIG. 135. *Detail of leno technique.*

FIG. 134. *A small wall hanging enhanced by a wide macramé fringe.*

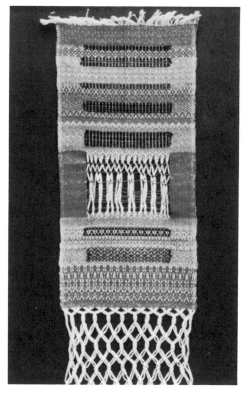

FIG. 136. *A wall hanging utilizing the leno technique with great decorative effectiveness.*

½ inch, the weft thread is passed across the open area to tie up the loose warp threads.

The last ½ inch of the hanging is woven with the same linen as the warp. This gives a firm edge. Before removing from the loom, this edge must be oversewn to prevent unravelling. Oversewing can be done by using overlapping stitches on the final few rows.

When the hanging is removed from the loom, tie the loose warp ends in groups of four, close to the bottom of the weaving. Pin the bottom of the hanging to a piece of wood clamped to a table or other suitable workplace. Next, make four rows (or more, if there is enough string) of loose mesh macramé knots. This loose mesh, if evenly done, looks like a pattern of flowers. Leave the remaining ends as a fringe but trim them evenly across.

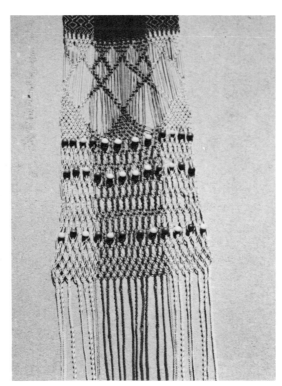

FIG. 137. *Colorful wooden beads add flair to this hanging finished with macramé.*

Second Woven Wall Hanging with Macramé

This warp is white on each side and green in the center. Again, it would work equally well in any other colors. And, the weft may aslo be woven in other colors. However, before you substitute your own color choices, draw a small picture with crayons or pencils to get an idea of what the colors will look like when they are juxtaposed. Fisherman's twine is used, and there are 200 ends. The hanging is 12 inches wide. An 8-dent reed is used with 2 threads in every dent. The loom is threaded in point draw: 1–2–3–4–3–2–1 repeated. This gives a diamond pattern when woven in even-sided twill: that is, you raise shafts 1 and 2, 2 and 3, 3 and 4, 4 and 1, and repeat. For the weft, jute is used. Four inches is woven in dark brown, 4 inches in red, and 4 inches in black. The work is then taken from the loom. The ends are divided into groups of four and tied very close to the bottom of the weaving with Square Knots.

The macramé pattern starts with small sennits of 3 knots each. The work is then shaped into diamonds surrounded by loose mesh knots. In the center of the diamond shapes, put small copper tubes. Into the large diamond, put transparent plastic tubes. After the large diamonds, introduce wooden beads in various colors. Continue knotting in loose mesh for 6 inches and then have another row of beads. Then have loose mesh for 4 inches and a last row of beads. Finish the wall hanging with rows of sennits and Spirals for 15 inches.

STOLES FINISHED WITH MACRAMÉ

Macramé makes a beautiful finish for a woven stole. This is done in a similar way to the wall hanging. Use a regular 15-dent reed. After having woven 1½ yards, take the stole off the loom. Unlike the wall hanging, both ends of the stole must be finished with macramé. Divide the leftover warp into groups of four threads and tie them close to the bottom of the weaving. Then make three or four rows of loose mesh macramé knots (see figure 139).

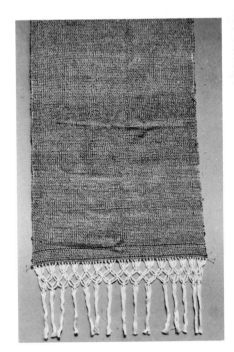

FIG. 138. *A woven stole beautifully finished with a macramé fringe.*

PART THREE

Tapestry and Double Weave

9

TAPESTRY
WEAVING

Introduction

TAPESTRY weaving is not as difficult a technique as might at first be presumed. The beautiful medieval tapestries which may be seen in museums, such as the Unicorn Tapestries in The Cloisters in New York, are in this respect misleading. They were, for the most part, made at very large looms by a number of workers working at the same time. The weavers were not the designers.

The same is true for the magnificent Lurçat tapestries. Jean Lurçat produced the cartoon and supervised the work, and his tapestries were woven in special workshops. Very fine modern tapestries made under similar conditions may be seen in the United Nations building in New York. Today, however, there are many artists who both design and weave their own tapestries.

THE LOOM

Tapestries can be woven on any kind of loom (simple or very complex): a frame loom, an upright loom, a 2-shaft loom, or a 4-shaft loom. This is because only two shafts are necessary for tapestry. For those new to weaving, a frame loom is suitable for your first experiments. Many expert tapestry weavers also use a frame loom simply because they prefer it.

FIG. 139. La Dame à la Licorne *(detail) from the Museum of Cluny, Paris, France. A sixteenth-century tapestry.*

FIG. 140. *Detail from a Jean Lurçat tapestry*, Le Bestiaire.

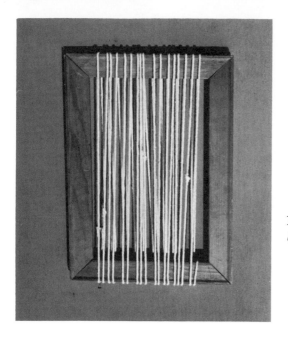

FIG. 141. *Frame loom that can be used for weaving tapestry.*

FIG. 142. *Two sticks are used to show weaving on a frame loom.*

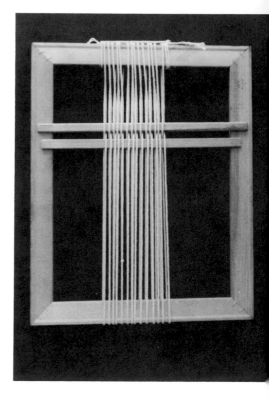

If you are using a frame loom, take a long piece of string or a spool of yarn. Nail or tie one end of the string to one corner of the frame. Wrap the string around the frame a number of times—the number depending on how wide you want your work to be. The string should not overlap, but each strand should be close to the preceding one. If you want your warp to be 6 inches wide, measure the distance from the beginning of the warp. Continue winding the string around the frame until you reach the 6-inch mark and then nail or tie the end of the string. When warping the frame, make sure you leave a space of one-eighth inch between each string. This forms the warp (fig. 142). If more advanced weavers use a frame loom by choice, they do not wind the warp around the outside of the frame. Instead, they fasten a series of nails to the frame and wind the warp around these. This, of course, results in a flatter warp which is easier to work with.

To weave the material on the frame loom, you must have the weft interlocking with the warp. Take a hand shuttle or a piece of cardboard, wind some yarn around it and go over the first warp thread, under the second, over the third, under the fourth and so on until you reach the end. When you arrive at the end, reverse the process, that is, go under the first and over the second, etc. Continue in this way until you have finished (fig. 143). If you wish to use two colors, use two shuttles

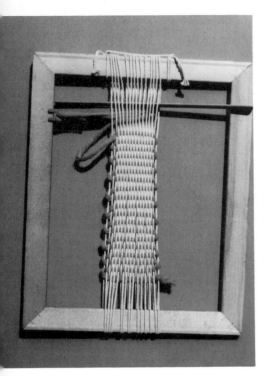

FIG. 143. *Weaving on a frame loom. Notice how the stick is used to form a shed for weaving.*

with a different color on each. One can be used to go from left to right, and the other from right to left.

An upright or high-warp loom is frequently used for tapestry. This is most often the case with professional tapestry artists. In weaving workshops, where a number of weavers work on the same tapestry, very large, high-warp looms are always used. While ideal for tapestry, an upright loom is otherwise limited in scope, and the majority of weavers will probably prefer to use the more versatile 4-shaft loom. Even a 20-inch table loom can make very fine tapestries which are only restricted as to their width.

DESIGN

Until the beginning of this century, tapestry designers tended to imitate oil painting—in other words, continuing the tradition of the French seventeenth and eighteenth-century tapestries. These tapestries were woven using a fine dent reed, allowing very detailed work, and with a vast array of colors. The great French artist Jean Lurçat was, more than anyone else, responsible for the rebirth of tapestry in this century. He broke completely with the old traditions and moved far away from the over-realistic and elaborate tapestries of the past. He reduced the number of dents per inch in the reed so that strong bold designs became possible. Then, he reduced the palette

FIG. 144. *Detail from the Jean Lurçat tapestry,* Le Bestiaire.

1 1 2

and worked with a smaller number of colors. As he said in his book, *Designing Tapestry*, "Tapestry only lives by strong values in juxtaposition, working by contrasts."[1]

Some weavers come to tapestry from painting, and for them, designing tapestries may present fewer problems than for those who feel that they are less creative. Inspiration can often be gained from modern paintings, both in overall design and in the use of color. Matisse, for example, has designed a number of tapestries, and many of his paintings would make admirable tapestries. Cubist works of Braque and Picasso—at a time when their paintings seemed very much alike—can also be a source of ideas for the tapestry weaver. We recommend a comparatively simple design, especially for those new to tapestry weaving. The tapestries shown on pages 114 (fig. 147) and 117 are effective but not too elaborate in their design.

1. Jean Lurçat, *Designing Tapestry* (London: Rockliff, 1950), p. 10.

FIG. 145. *A tapestry, striking but simple in design—ideal for the beginner in tapestry weaving.*

A tapestry should be very carefully planned before the weaving is begun. Experienced tapestry weavers use a cartoon which they prepare before starting work, but even the beginner should make some preliminary sketches. It is advisable to make several and then choose the best. It is probably most satisfactory to make your first sketches in black and white, concentrating on the overall design and aiming at a balanced composition.

After you have decided on the basic design, you should then plan the colors, taking into account the available yarns. It is a good idea to color the sketches, partly because when weaving a tapestry on a floor loom, one sometimes forgets which colors have been used at an earlier stage of the work, and the colored sketches can be particularly helpful in this respect. Far more important is the question of the whole composition of the tapestry, in which color plays a vital part.

The next question to be decided is the size of the tapestry. Here the weaver must, to a certain extent, be guided by the size of the available loom. Even with a 40-inch loom, it is not advisable to make a tapestry wider than 35 inches. At this point, the weaver should decide whether the tapestry is to be woven sideways or from bottom to top. On a narrow loom, of course, it is not possible to weave the tapestry sideways. If you have

FIG. 147. Market Girl, *by the author, shows how vitally important color is in the overall composition.*

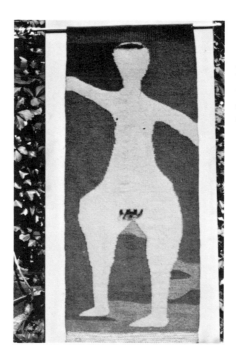

FIG. 146. *The design for this tapestry was first sketched on paper by the weaver.*

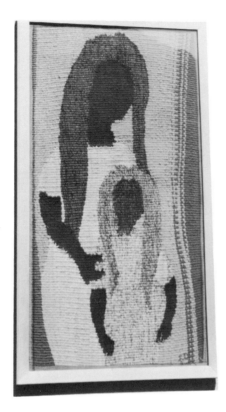

FIG. 148. *This tapestry, predominantly of vertical lines, was woven sideways.*

a larger loom, and your design has a large number of vertical lines, then weave it sideways. If, on the other hand, the lines are horizontal rather than vertical, weave the tapestry the right way up.

The next step is to transfer your design to the cartoon. Brown wrapping paper is quite suitable for this, as it is strong enough to withstand being wound together with the warp. The cartoon must be the exact size of the tapestry. Most weavers prefer to color their cartoons, reproducing the colors that they will use as closely as possible. Tempera or watercolors can be used for this. Other weavers do not color their cartoons at all, but number the various sections to correspond with their yarns.

MATERIALS

When planning materials, you must also decide how many dents per inch to use. You can use a 12-dent reed or even a 15-dent reed, but in the latter case, you must use a fine yarn. You can then also use a more elaborate design. Today's artist-craftsman usually prefers an 8-dent reed: not only can heavier yarns be used, but the resulting tapestry is more in accordance with modern ideas of design.

You can use either linen or cotton for the warp. Linen is longer-lasting, and for this reason, is preferred by many professional weavers. With an 8-dent reed you would use either 16-ply or 30-ply cotton. With a 12-dent reed, 6 or 10-ply cotton can be used.

For the weft yarn, 2-ply or 3-ply wool is very suitable. Knitting wool can also be used, and oddments can be used up in this way. Haitian hand-spun natural cotton blends well with wool and adds an interesting texture. For a design which relies for its effect mainly on large blocks of color, a thick tapestry yarn can be used as in the tapestry shown in figure 150.

PREPARATIONS FOR WEAVING

If you are planning a 30-inch by 36-inch tapestry, it is recommended that you make a warp long enough for two or three tapestries. You could use the first part of your warp for a sampler, if this is your first attempt at tapestry. In this way you can master some of the necessary techniques before you start work on your first really creative piece of weaving.

In tapestry weaving, the weft covers the warp completely, and the design is therefore made entirely by the weft. To attain this end, you weave by alternately raising shafts 1 and 2 and shafts 3 and 4 on a 4-shaft loom (1 and 2 alternately on a 2-shaft loom). The beating process is of very great importance in tapestry weaving. If not done correctly, the warp is still visible. The beater can be used if the weft is in a straight line, but as soon as you start making the design and introducing curves and different colors, it is no longer possible to use the beater. Some people use a comb for the beating, but I personally find a regular table fork more satisfactory. With the fork, you beat the weft so close that the warp threads are completely covered. The tapestry is made in such a way that it has only one side, and the wrong side has a large number of loose ends. When you start your design, the different colors are wound onto small shuttles, 3 inches to 4 inches long. These can be cut from heavy cardboard and should have the shape of the shuttle illustrated in figure 149.

FIG. 149. *A shuttle. Each different color used requires one of these.*

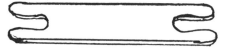

As previously suggested, it is recommended that you acquire some of the techniques necessary for tapestry weaving by making a sampler before you start on your first tapestry. The sampler can be of any form you choose but should be made of at least two different colors woven in blocks with horizontal, vertical, and diagonal lines between them. The rug shown in figure 150 was woven to learn tapestry techniques. Your sampler can, of course, be much smaller and simpler than this.

FIG. 150. *This rug incorporates in its design the various tapestry-weaving techniques.*

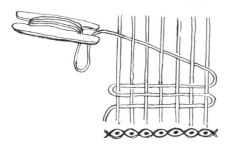

FIG. 151. *This drawing illustrates the method of weaving horizontally.*

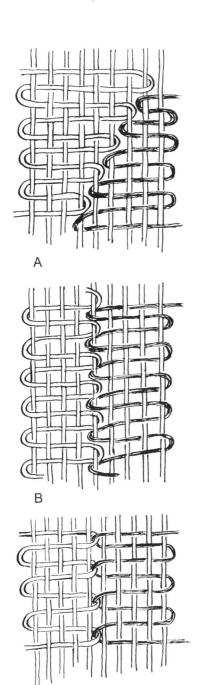

A

B

C

TAPESTRY TECHNIQUES

Horizontal lines offer no problem, as they are simply woven straight across, raising shafts 1 and 2 and shafts 3 and 4 alternately. Horizontal stripes of varying widths can thus be woven very easily, as the colors can be changed at will.

A vertical, striped effect can be obtained by using two colors on different shuttles. One color is woven from right to left, and the other from left to right. After a few picks, the direction can be changed. You will then have a pattern as at the end of the rug in figure 150.

The diagonal line, which is of great importance in tapestry weaving, is very simple to do. Start with one color on each side. Move one color in a diagonal line to the left, by weaving around one extra warp thread each pick. At the same time, the other color is woven around one less thread each time. This makes a fairly sharp diagonal line. For a more sloping line, weave around two extra threads each pick. If, on the other hand, you want your diagonal line to have a very steep angle, weave around one extra thread on every other pick, and not on every pick. (See figure 152–A.)

Vertical lines are not as easily made as horizontal or diagonal lines. For this reason, one often finds on primitive tapestries that vertical lines are completely avoided. This is not to be recommended, however, since if there are no vertical lines, the weaver is very much restricted in choice of design. Vertical lines are most easily made by either dovetailing or interlocking.

1. Dovetailing. This is done as in figure 152–B. The two colors (one from the right; one from the left) meet in the middle and both go around the same warp thread. For example, you take your red thread from the left, weave it around the warp thread and then return it to the left side. Next, take your blue thread from the right, and weave it around the same warp thread. In this way, no gap will be formed.

2. Interlocking. In this method, the two weft threads, when meeting in the middle, are wound around each other before being returned to their respective sides. They are not wound around the same warp thread. (See figure 152–C.)

3. Slit. In this method, the two colors are not joined in the middle and do not go around the same warp thread. As a result, there is a slit between the two colors. This is normally sewn up later. If you examine medieval or Renaissance tapestries in museums, you will see many examples of this method. In certain tapestries, the slit is used to form a deliberate part of the design. (See figure 152–D.)

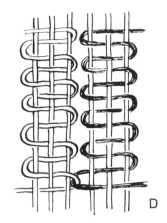

FIG. 152. *Tapestry weaving techniques: diagonal (A), dovetail (B), interlocking (C), slit (D).*

WEAVING THE TAPESTRY

To start your tapestry, weave about 6 inches to 8 inches plain weave. Then begin to use tapestry technique in a straight line in one or two colors. You are still able to use the beater at this point. After about 3 inches to 4 inches, start your actual design. The first step is to pin your cartoon underneath your warp to the part which you have already woven. Start following the design according to the cartoon.

Many weavers find it difficult to keep the sides of their tapestries in a straight line. Straight sides depend first on the correct even tension of the warp, and second on the way the tapestry is woven. It is important to start weaving the design in the center and work toward the sides. Above all, the warp thread should never be pulled. The weft threads should also not be pulled too tight. The weft threads should be taken very lightly around the warp threads, so that the latter stay in a completely straight line. (See figure 153).

When you have a curved shape, you build it up from the middle toward the left and from the middle toward the right. This helps keep the warp tension even and the sides straight. You should, in any case, never allow any one part of your design to be built up too far beyond the rest. When weaving your tapestry, use the techniques learned in making your sampler. Follow your cartoon exactly. When making a curved line or a circle, use dovetailing or interlocking to keep the line of your cartoon. You should always remember to change the shed, so that you do not have two parallel threads in the same shed.

FIG. 153. *This drawing shows the right and wrong way of pulling a weft thread around a warp thread.*

FINISHING THE TAPESTRY

Weave about two inches in one color to finish off the tapestry. Some weavers prefer to sew the edge before removing from the loom, but it can also be sewn afterward. If the yarn is not too thick, you may hem the sides if you wish. Some people line their tapestries, but this is not usually necessary. It is often advisable to block the work and then press it with a hot iron and a damp cloth.

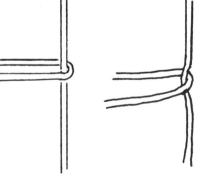

Correct   Incorrect

119

Hooking is one of the easiest methods of making a tapestry, wall hanging, or rug. It is possible to buy a special hooking loom, but you can also use an artist's stretcher, according to the size your piece is going to be. You staple the material onto the stretcher, as you would a canvas. The material usually used for hooking is monk's cloth, but you can also experiment with burlap. Hooking is done with a special hooking needle, obtainable at any arts and crafts supply store.

Draw your design on top of the material, then thread your hooking needle and follow the pattern. Change the color of the thread when needed. Always start hooking from the center of your piece and work out toward the sides. After you have finished your work, it is recommended that you apply a coat of liquid rubber to the back to keep the threads together, so that the tapestry does not unravel.

Fig. 154. *A tapestry utilizing the hooking method.*

Rug technique can be used for different purposes—that is, for rugs, tapestries, or wall hangings. It is always best to weave from 10 inches to 12 inches of plain weave before you start your rug. It is possible to use a 6-dent reed, an 8-dent reed, or a 12-dent reed. However, on a 12-dent reed, you would have to use fine yarn for your rug.

The knotting process is very easy. Before you start, you cut the knotting yarn into 3-inch to 4-inch lengths. The knot used is the Giordes knot which is tied as in figure 155. On a 4-shaft loom, raise shafts 1 and 2. Lay the yarn over the first two warp threads and pass the left-hand end under the left warp thread and up between the two threads. The right-hand end is passed under the right warp thread, and again up between the two warp threads. The two ends are then pulled tight. Proceed in this way right across your warp. Then, weave either two or four rows of plain weave to secure the knot before repeating the knotting process. A design can be planned as for a tapestry. You can follow your design either with a cartoon, as previously described, or with a sketch or by painting the warp threads.

This technique is admirably suited for making rugs but can also be used to make very attractive wall hangings. Figure 156 is an illustration of a tapestry made with this technique. If you do not want a flat surface, your knots can be cut to different lengths. Many weavers combine rug techniques with other forms of weaving. An example is Yvonne Forbach's *Fertile Earth* (fig. 157).

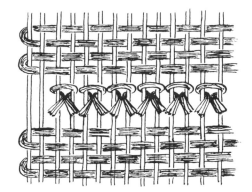

FIG. 155. *The Giordes knot is used in tapestry weaving to give the work textured appearance.*

FIG. 156. *A wall hanging utilizing the Giordes knot.*

FIG. 157. Fertile Earth. *Yvonne Forbach.*

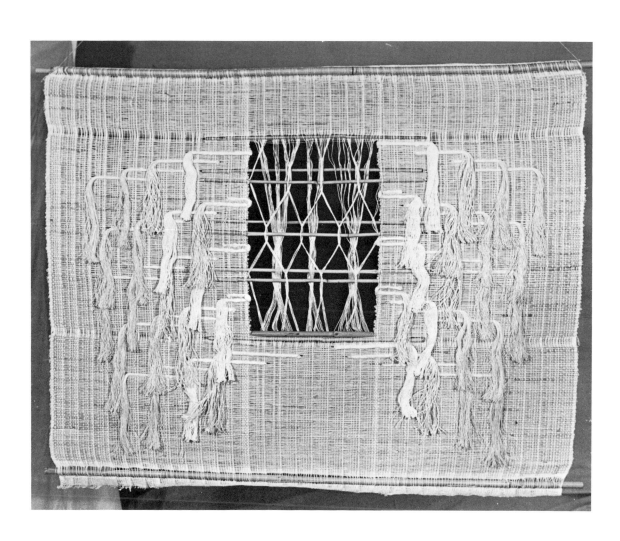

10

WALL HANGINGS IN DOUBLE WEAVE

ALL weavers interested in wall hangings should master the art of double weave. To get an idea of the different effects which can be obtained with this technique you may want to study figures 158 and 160. These two wall hangings, which have little or no resemblance to each other, were woven from the same warp and are both made using the double-weave technique. Some spectacular designs can be made with double weave, and double weave is a technique that is far simpler than you would imagine.

DOUBLE-WEAVE CLOTH

Double cloth consists of two separate layers of fabric that are woven on the same warp: a tubular material would result if the two layers were woven completely separately, apart from being joined at the two outer sides. However, such a tubular material is not suitable for wall hangings. In order to make a fairly firm hanging, the two layers should be joined at intervals of not more than three inches. With a straight draw and

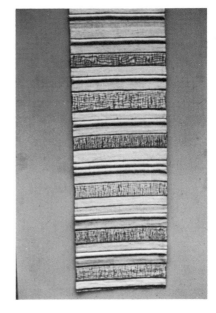

FIG. 158. *Double-weave wall hanging. Rosalind Dépas.*

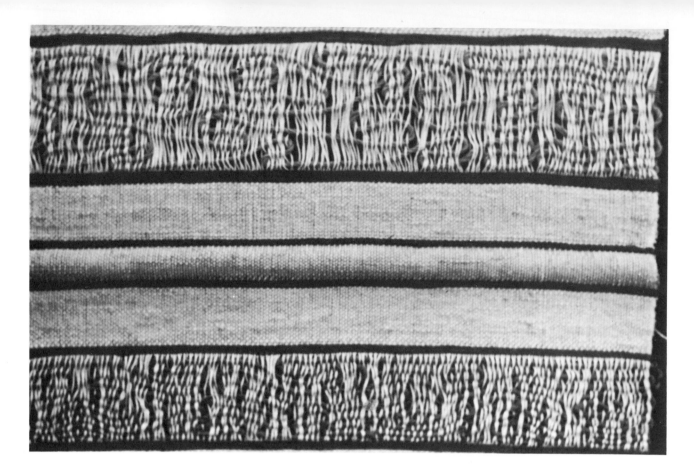

FIG. 159. *Detail of double-weave cloth.*

two threads per dent, double cloth will be produced by the following method.

For the lower layer, raise shafts 2, 3, and 4 followed by shafts 1, 2, and 4. For the upper layer, raise shafts 2 and 4 alternately. If different colors are used for the two layers, interesting color effects can be obtained.

To join the layers, a band of plain weave should be woven every few inches (by raising shafts 1 and 3; 2 and 4). Two or four rows will be sufficient to make the material firm.

First Wall Hanging in Double Weave

This is a very suitable wall hanging for the weaver anxious to learn the technique of double cloth. It is simple and quick to make but very effective. The hanging measures 18 inches by 52 inches. The warp is made with two cotton threads—one white, one green. As we are using a 14 dent reed with two threads per dent (i.e., 28 ends per inch) we shall need a total of 504 ends + 2 selvage, that is 506 ends. As in other projects you can substitute any colors you wish for the ones that are suggested. I've left the color references because I think it makes the directions easier to follow. If you use other colors, make a chart similar to the one shown here, but listing the threads in your color choices. The loom is threaded in straight draw, but in such a way that for the most part, only the white threads appear on the upper surface. This is done as follows:

---

thread shaft 1 white
thread shaft 2 green
thread shaft 3 white
thread shaft 4 green

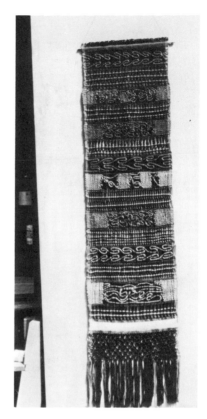

FIG. 160. *First wall hanging in double weave.*

FIG. 161. *Detail of first wall hanging in double weave.*

1 2 5

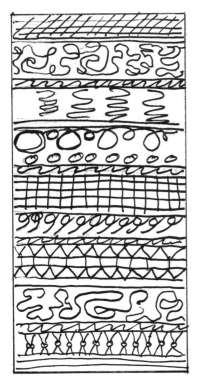

Fig. 162. *Plans for first wall hanging in double weave.*

In each dent there is one white thread and one green thread.

The weft is made of linen thread in pale blue, dark blue, pink, and green. The hanging is made of alternating bands of plain weave and double weave. In some of the bands of double cloth, tubular wadding ¾-inch thick[1] is inserted to give an interesting raised effect. Other bands are left flat. The bands with the wadding insertion should not be too wide, so that they will be firm. About one inch would be suitable. If narrower, it would be difficult to fit the wadding. If wider, the wadding would not fill up the empty space. It is recommended that as you weave, you should try the wadding to see if it fits.

The bands of different colors and techniques should be of varying widths to avoid monotony. You can start with a band of pale blue double cloth about 2 inches wide. Follow this with 4 rows plain weave in dark blue. Your next band should be pink for insertion. For this raised band, when you have woven 1 inch of double cloth, place the wadding between the two layers. Push it well down so that it fits tightly, and then join the two layers with four rows of plain weave in dark blue. On this hanging, all the joining bands of plain weave are in dark blue.

Make one more band pale blue and follow this with a pink band for insertion. After one more 2-inch pale blue band, you may try something more ambitious. This is a variant of Spanish lace technique. Weave 3 inches of the bottom layer in green; that is, by raising shafts 2, 3, and 4 and shafts 1, 2, and 4. The upper threads—the white ones—will be left lying loose on top of the darker background. When the bottom layer is completed, you are then going to work with the loose upper warp threads.

Thread a short shuttle (not more than 6 inches) with a contrasting wool or other heavy yarn. This is then woven backward and forward over a few warp threads at a time to make an interesting scrolled and curved pattern. Use a fork as a beater in order to put the yarn in exactly the right position according to your design. Try to do this as evenly as possible so as not to leave any large spaces without pattern.

In this hanging, the first Spanish lace design is made with dark blue wool. Then, after another raised section with pale blue double-weave bands on each side, there follows a wider Spanish lace band. This is 4 inches wide and is made with pink wool. The following Spanish lace design is again of dark blue

1. Obtainable from drapery stores and yarn suppliers.

wool but this time more closely woven. As a result, the blue stands out, whereas the white warp threads in the first Spanish lace band overshadow the blue weft threads.

After this, the design changes slightly. The next raised section is double—that is, after the first wadding insertion there are four rows of plain weave as before, and then immediately another pink raised section. As before, the next Spanish lace section is pink with pale blue on each side. Then, the colors change, so that the flat double cloth is now in pink, and the raised sections are in pale blue. One more dark blue Spanish lace section and one pink Spanish lace band complete the wall hanging.

The hanging we have described is approximately 52 inches long but can, of course, be made to any desired length by alternating different bands of techniques and colors. You can control the length of any piece of weaving by measuring from the start of your work and pinning a piece of paper (with the length written on it) to the side of your work. When you wind on your warp, measure from the spot you have pinned and pin a piece of paper with the new measurement near the end of your work. In this way you will control the length of your work. Do not forget, however, that you are measuring the stretched warp, and when it is removed from the loom, it will be shorter.

Second Wall Hanging in Double Weave

The next two wall hangings in double weave are made from the same warp. As in the first wall hanging, use the colors that you think are most attractive. If you use your own colors, it is a good idea to make a working chart listing the new colors and describing each operation with the color you wish to use. This kind of chart should be near the loom, where you can use it while working. The warp is 16 inches wide and 6 yards long, which is ample for two wall hangings—one 65 inches long, with a deep macramé fringe, and the other 38 inches long. A 10-dent reed is used so that there are 20 ends per inch. Allowing for 4 selvage threads each side, you have a total of 328 ends. Black cotton is used for the warp, with 16 ends of purple cotton on each side. The warp is threaded in straight draw.

The first section of the wall hanging is woven in cotton, with red cotton used for the lower layer and yellow cotton for the

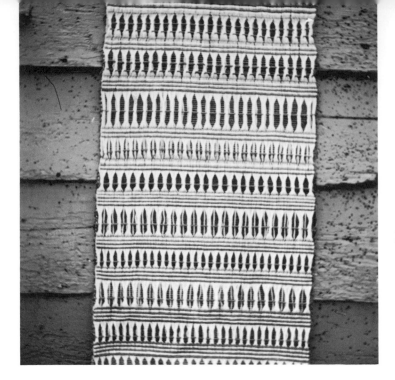

FIG. 163. *Second wall hanging
in double weave.*

upper layer. In other words, raise shafts 1, 2, and 4 and 2, 3,
and 4 for the red weft; raise shafts 2 and 4 alternately for the
yellow weft.

After this, the pattern starts. Bands of leno alternate with
bands of Spanish lace. Cotton is used throughout for the background—that is, for the lower layer, which, at least in the
leno sections, shows through quite clearly. The patterns are
woven in a fairly thick yarn.

First, weave 2½ inches of red cotton background. For the
leno pattern, a stick is used to cross the threads over. Count
8 threads, pass the second 4 over the first 4, and put a stick
through. Do this right across the warp and then pull the orange
weft yarn through the intersections made by the stick. Next,
reverse the process in the other direction.

The first Spanish lace pattern is woven against a 4-inch red
cotton background, using the same orange yarn for the raised
pattern. Blocks of solid color about 2 inches wide are woven
on each side, and the center section is woven in Spanish lace.
Do not weave the side sections to the full height of the background all at one time. Weave about 1 inch on the right side.
Make a Spanish lace pattern to the same height in the center,
and then weave the solid section on the left to about the same
height. Afterward, you fill in the middle again and weave the
side sections, until the pattern is of the same height as the
background.

The bands of leno are woven by crossing and interlacing the black warp threads in various different ways. On the third band, for example, over a yellow background, four lines of blue are used to form a regular squared effect. On the fourth leno band, only two lines of pink yarn are used over a blue background. The groups of black warp threads, however, are crossed over between the two pink lines.

The Spanish lace sections consist sometimes of regular curved shapes—as in the second Spanish lace band, which has yellow weft yarn scrolled over a black background—to form a balanced pattern. In other patterns, blocks of solid color alternate with irregular Spanish lace designs.

The alternating leno and Spanish lace woven on black warp threads make a particularly effective wall hanging. This also offers the weaver great scope for varying the patterns that have been suggested.

When the hanging is finished, a narrow band of double weave is woven: this is used to insert the rod on which to hang the work.

Put in warp sticks before beginning the next hanging.

When the hanging is removed from the loom, the spare warp from the beginning of the hanging is used to make a wide macramé fringe. The warp threads are grouped eight at a time and then tightly knotted together. These groups of threads are then knotted in loose mesh to form as many rows of Square Knots as possible. The black warp threads knotted in macramé are very effective against a light wall.

FIG. 164. *Third wall hanging in double weave.*

Third Wall Hanging in Double Weave

Your third wall hanging in double weave—the second wall hanging made on this warp—at first glance has the appearance of a tapestry but is actually made in double weave. A preliminary sketch was made for this hanging, but a cartoon was not used. The sides of the hanging are woven, while the central black figure consists of unwoven or floating warp threads. As in the other double-weave wall hangings, it is necessary to weave one or two sheds of plain weave every few inches. Otherwise, it is difficult to control the loose warp threads in the center which, in any case, tend to be a little difficult to handle. To keep the proportions correct, the sketch was drawn to a scale of 4 to 1. In other words, if on the sketch there was a curve to

FIG. 165. *Original rough sketch*
of wall hanging.

FIG. 166. *Detail of sketch work.*

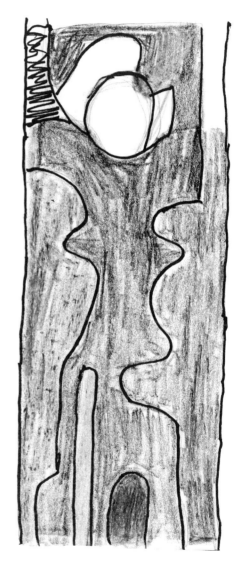

130

FIG. 167. *Completed sketch for use in weaving finished work.*

FIG. 168. *A red leno wall hanging, 10 feet long and 24 inches wide.*

the left after 1 inch, this curve was woven after approximately 4 inches. In this type of hanging, as long as the main proportions are kept in mind, the design can be varied to a certain extent as weaving progresses.

Conclusion

In *Macramé, Weaving, and Tapestry*, I have tried to tell you about three textile art forms that are similar. They are similar because they all use textile as a medium, and they are all built on a series of vertical threads—the ends (for macramé) and the warp (for weaving and tapestry).

Because of textures and three-dimensional forms that can evolve from macramé, it can be exciting in a one-color twine. Weaving, with its more subtle textures, can be combined effectively with macramé in either a monochromatic or colorful design. Tapestry largely depends on the use of color for its effect and impact.

I hope this book will start you on an exploration into my favorite form of textile art—large macramé wall hangings.

Glossary

Beater. Frame to hold reed. This separates the warp threads and is used to beat the weft.

Bobbins. Also called *quills,* they hold the weft thread and fit inside the shuttle.

Dent. A single space in a reed through which the warp is threaded. The reed is classified according to the number of dents to an inch (e.g., *10-dent reed* means a reed with ten dents per inch).

Double Weave. Also called double cloth, it is a form of weaving in which there are two separate layers woven on one warp.

Dovetailing. A technique in tapestry weaving in which the weft threads go around the same warp thread so that they are interlocked.

Four-Harness Loom. A loom with four harnesses or shafts. More elaborate patterns can be woven with a loom of this type than with the simpler two-shaft loom.

Frame Loom. A primitive loom without heddles or beaters.

Giordes Knot. A knot used in making rugs.

Heddles. Vertical strings or wires hung in the harness to hold the warp threads.

Heddle Eye. An opening in the center of the heddle through which the warp is threaded.

High Warp Loom. A vertical loom used for tapestry or rug weaving.

Hooking. A rug technique in which yarn is knotted with a special needle on a canvas base.

Interlocking. A method of joining colors in tapestry weaving in which the threads are wound around each other.

Leno. An open lace weave with twisted warp threads.

Loom. Apparatus used for weaving fabric.

Macramé. A type of Square Knotting formerly used by sailors.

Pick. A single throw of weft thread.

Plain Weave. The simplest form of weaving. The weft threads pass alternately over and under successive warp threads.

Reed. The comb-like part of the beater used to separate warp threads.

Rug Technique. Any method of weaving or hooking suitable for making rugs.

Sampler. A small piece of weaving for learning new techniques.

Selvage. The edge of a woven fabric.

Shaft. The harness or frame hanging from the upper part of the loom to hold the heddles.

Shed. The opening in the warp threads through which the shuttle is passed. The shed is made by raising one or more shafts.

Shuttle. Tool used for carrying the weft thread through the shed. On a small loom or for tapestry work, this is usually flat and made of either fiber or wood. For a larger loom, this is usually boat-shaped with a removable bobbin.

Tabby. Another name for plain weave.

Tapestry Weave. A variation of plain weave sometimes known as rib weave. Straight draw is used, and shafts 1 and 2, 3 and 4 are raised alternately.

Transposed Weave. A form of reversed twill.

Twill. A form of weaving in which the weft threads form a diagonal pattern.

Warp. The threads that run lengthwise in the loom.

Warp Chain. The chain formed with the warp threads after they are removed from the warping reel.

Warping Reel. A revolving frame for making warps.

Warp Stick. A long stick used to hold the cross in the warp before threading.

Weaving. Interlacing yarns to form fabric.

Weft. Threads woven across warp threads to form fabric.

Weft twill. A twill weave in which the weft predominates.

Zigzag twill. A variation of twill which forms a zigzag pattern.

Bibliography

Alexander, Marthann. *Simple Weaving*. New York: Taplinger, 1968.

Anchor Manual of Needlework. 3d ed. Newton Center, Mass.: Charles T. Branford Co., 1968.

Ashley, Clifford W. *The Ashley Book of Knots*. Garden City, N.Y.: Doubleday, 1944.

Atwater, Mary Meigs. *Byways in Handweaving*. New York: Macmillan, 1968.

Black, Mary. *New Key to Weaving*. New York: Macmillan, 1961.

De Dillmont, Therese. *Encyclopedia of Needlework*. rev. ed. New York: DMC Library, 1971.

"Dictionary of Macramé" [and directions for making sixteen items]. *Woman's Day*, July 1969, pp. 40-43.

Good Housekeeping Needlecraft. New York: Hearst Corporation, 1969.

Graumont, Raoul, and Hensel, John. *Encyclopedia of Knots and Fancy Rope Work*. 4th ed. Cambridge, Md.: Cornell Maritime Press, 1952.

Graumont, Raoul, and Wenstrom, Elmer. *Square Knot Handicraft Guide*. Cambridge, Md.: Cornell Maritime Press, 1949.

Hartung, Rolf. *Creative Textile Design*. New York: Van Nostrand Reinhold Co., 1964.

Harvey and Tidball. *Weft Twining*. Pacific Groves, Calif.: Craft and Hobby Book Service, 1969.

Harvey, Virginia. *The Art of Creative Knotting*. New York: Van Nostrand Reinhold Co., 1967.

Herwig, Philip C., Sr. *Square Knot Booklet #1, #2, #3*. 3d ed. New York: Philip C. Herwig, Sr., 1926.

Oelsner, G. H. *Handbook of Weaves*. rev. ed. Edited by Samuel S. Dale. New York: Dover, 1952.

Pesch, Imelda M. *Macramé Bags*. Jackson Heights, N.Y.: Pesch Art Studio, 1964.

Philips, Mary Walker. *Step-by-Step Macramé*. New York: Golden Press, 1970.

Suppliers

Loom and Loom Accessories

Bailey Manufacturing Co.
118 Lee Street
Lodi, Ohio 44252

Bradshaw Manufacturing Co.
P.O. Box 425
West Columbia, S.C. 29169

Craftool Company
1 Industrial Road
Woodbridge, N.J. 07075

The Handcrafters
521 W. Brown Street
Waupun, Wis. 53963

Loomcraft Studio
678 Rombach Avenue
Wilmington, Ohio

Nadeau Looms, Inc.
725 Branch Avenue
Providence, R.I.

Dyes—Vegetable

Catherine Morony
Penland, N.C.

Keyston Ingham
8726 E. Cleta
Downey, Calif.

Museum of Northern Arizona
Flagstaff, Arizona

Dyes—Synthetic

Berry's of Maine
20–22 Main Street
Yarmouth, Maine

CIBA Chemical & Dye Co.
Fairlawn, N.J.

Merck & Company, Ltd.
Rahway, N.H.

7K Color Company
927 Citrus Street
Hollywood, Calif.

Yarns

Linen Yarns

Frederick J. Fawcett, Inc.
129 South Street
Boston, Mass. 02111

William and Company
Box 318
Madison Square Station
New York, N.Y. 10010

Wool Yarns

Paternayan Bros., Inc.
312 East Ninety-Fifth Street
New York, N.Y. 10038

William Condon & Sons Ltd.
65 Queen Street
Charlottetown, P.O. Box 129
Prince Edward Island, Canada

Assorted Yarns, Threads, and Embroidery

The Artisans Guild, Inc.
Box 42
Cambridge, Mass. 02138

Dick Blick
P.O. Box 1267
Galesburg, Ill. 61401

CCM Arts and Crafts, Inc.
9520 Baltimore Avenue
College Park, Md. 20740

Contessa Yarns
P.O. Box 37
Lebanon, Conn. 06249

Craft Yarns of Rhode Island, Inc.
603 Mineral Spring Avenue
Rhode Island 02862

Creative Hands Co., Inc.
4146 Library Road
Pittsburgh, Pa. 15234

Economy Handicrafts Inc.
47 – 11 Francis-Lewis Blvd.
Flushing, N.Y. 11361

Frederick J. Fawcett, Inc.
129 South Street
Boston, Mass. 02111

William and Company
Box 318
Madison Square Station
New York, N.Y. 10010

The Yarn Depot (also T pins)
545 Sutter Street
San Francisco, Calif. 94102

Buckles, Rings, and T Pins

Greenberg & Hammer, Inc.
24 West Fifty-Seventh Street
New York, N.Y. 10022

P.C. Herwig Co.
264 Clinton Street
Brooklyn, N.Y. 11201

Scovill Manufacturing Co.
Oakville Division
350 Fifth Avenue
New York, N.Y. 10001

Walco Toy Co., Inc.
38 West Thirty-Seventh Street
New York, N.Y. 10018

Index

143